Crime and Punishment: D

Author Page

Susan Thomas lives in Oxford.

She graduated with an Honours degree in Psychology with Statistics, and has a Masters degree in Criminology.

Table of Contents

This book is 30, 000 words long.

Introduction:

Prisons have been a tried and tested means of enacting criminal justice for many centuries. These days the sentences are far more lenient than those imposed in days gone by. Between the seventeenth to nineteenth centuries there was a draconian severity in the punishment of British prisoners. There were over two hundred petty crimes that could be punishable by hanging. This became the time known as the Bloody Code in sentencing. These days many people think that the pendulum has swung too far in the opposite direction and that life is too cushy for prison inmates. The public feel aggrieved to see pictures posted by inmates in British prisons where they are smoking joint s of cannabis and appear to be having lot of fun!

Conditions seem to be far stricter in American jails and the supermax prisons are well known for their maximum security conditions. This is in stark contrast to a British prison where there have been documented cases of drones flying over the prison walls carrying a delivery of drugs to the inmates!

The American criminal justice system holds more than **2.3 million** people in **1,719** state prisons, 102 federal prisons, 942 juvenile correctional facilities, 3,283 local jails, and 79 Indian Country jails as well as in military prisons, immigration detention facilities, civil commitment centers, and prisons in the U.S.

By contrast there are around 83, 000 male inmates in British jails and only 3800 female inmates. There is no more room to take any more inmates in British jails. Since the prisons are over crowded the sentencing guidelines are being changed to accommodate this fact. This means that many offenders are now routinely given probation or community orders in order to avoid adding to the problem of over crowded prisons.

Chapter One: Powerful Criminals Evade Prison

Society is inevitably hierarchical. This premise seems to apply to the world of crime and punishment. It is often the case that very rich and powerful corporations and individuals are able to evade the tawdry world of prison.

Criminals wear many masks. The archetypal mask of Highwayman Dick Turpin, worn by modern day assailants such as burglars and hoodies epitomises the public perception of dangerous street criminals. However a vast amount of crime is cloaked in an expensive suit of respectability and legitimate authority rather than a bandit` s mask. This invisible cloak of crime is worn by respectable corporations who can inflict serious yet indirect damage on society and its component individuals. Given the arbitrary nature of the definition of crime as well as the privileged status of those who define it this essay will proceed to delineate the relationship between crimes of the powerful as opposed to the more common petty street crime that frequently hits the headlines.

This chapter will delineate some of the ingenious crimes committed by respected institutions such as banks, pharmaceutical companies, elected politicians and respected institutions and corporations in which the public often place a misguided trust. It will conclude that we must remain ever vigilant of legitimate authority, including the police and State, in order to protect ourselves. Just as we would take reasonable precautions to protect ourselves from street crimes such as muggings and burglary so we should critically regard the respectable institutions that form the bedrock of our society as being the potential perpetrators of invisible crime. This chapter will delineate the relationship between crimes of the powerful as opposed to the more common street crimes such as muggings that usually hit the headlines.

For instance it has been calculated by the Audit Commission that each and every family in this country will eventually pay in the region of £40,000 towards the bailout of the reckless banks that were bailed out during the recent 2008 banking crisis. A handbag snatcher or street mugger would rarely escape with such a vast sum! Such sophisticated malfeasance is understandably hard to quantify and pin down and yet it yields extremely high dividends in comparison to the low dividends yielded by common street crime.

Criminals come in all shapes and sizes and from every strata of society. Status driven acquisitive crime has been discussed in many studies including those on corporate or workplace crime. The term "white collar crime" refers to this type of crime and was first coined by Edwin Sutherland in 1939. At the time this was a very new and exciting concept as it had previously suited the wealthy genteel Edwardians to look down upon the impoverished criminal classes.

This enabled the ruling elite to exert control over the proletariat rabble and thereby protect their financial interests. This idea of inherent privilege was also examined at length in the radical works of Marx and Engels. Karl Marx felt that wealthy capitalists exploited the lower classes. It suited the elite plutocracy to label the poor as bad. Laws of the land may be construed as the normative structure of the dominant group.

Thus we have a criminal justice system that is replete with Justices and Magistrates emanating from a background of privilege and wealth. The seminal study by Edwin Sutherland helped bring about a shift and a change of perception. Criminals it seems could be ordinary and hardworking respectable individuals who dress smartly for work in a white collar shirt and a neat suit. They attract little attention since they are legitimately at the scene of the crime in contrast to a trespassing house breaker.

According to routine activity theorists the propensity to criminal behaviour is normal and driven by opportunism and an easy target . This theory may explain why recorded crime rose during the last century as prosperity grew bringing more opportunities. Routine activity theory also sits well with the incidence of occupational and corporate crime where temptation is ubiquitous .

As well as the individual acting alone, the company as a separate entity can act in a criminal way. Studies on group polarisation known as the "risky shift" might explain why such corporate groups behave recklessly as in the case of the fatal Challenger decision. Sutherland discusses criminal acts by American utilities companies such as General Electric in his book on white collar crime. Clearly these sharp business practices are motivated by greed rather than need. Indeed since white collar criminals are in employment they cannot use the excuse of pressing poverty for their actions.

Enron and power cuts:

A more recent case of corporate crime was the Enron scandal that erupted in 2001 in America that involved power cut malpractice with utility companies. Enron was a hugely successful company and listed by Fortune Magazine as being the most innovative company from 1996-2001. Enron employed a creative accountant, Andrew Fastow, who used numerous tricks to hide Enron` s liabilities. This seemingly robust company encouraged investors to buy shares in a company that was in fact hiding huge liabilities.

The dishonesty of Enron was not confined to its creative accounting techniques. Enron had given large donations to the political campaign of a Californian Senator, Phil Gramm, who was duly elected. In return he passed legislation in 2000 to deregulate electricity commodities. This was beneficial to Enron who owned many power utilities. Following the legislation California had 38 serious rolling blackout power cuts. These were engineered by Enron to maximise profits.

Any one power cut can seriously endanger life since power is essential for hospitals. This wholly unacceptable behaviour of corporations has been discussed by Stephen Box who asserts that one is seven times more likely to be killed by corporate negligence than a common street criminal .

A concerned whistle blower came forward in 2001. Investors rushed to dump their shares. A white knight rescue attempt by another company failed and Enron filed for bankruptcy.

Asil Nadir and Polly Peck:

Another high profile case in the U. K. was that of the Polly Peck Company. This large concern was owned by tycoon Asil Nadir. He allegedly fleeced investors of millions of pounds and then fled the country to escape justice. He has recently returned to face justice, hoping that the current Government will assist a once generous Tory donor. The SFO have been preparing a case against him.
The wealthy tycoon was tagged and had to obey a strict curfew in his penthouse apartment. One may speculate that some of the perpetrators of outrageous financial crimes might have suffered extreme deprivation as children resulting in poor self control.

An industry that is rife with corruption is the Pharmaceutical industry. In 2002 The Serious Fraud office launched an eight year long investigation into five drug companies known as Operation Holbein. More than a million computer drives and files were seized from the homes and offices of the six companies involved. The police arrived with search warrants for six pharmaceutical companies but no arrests were made.

The six companies accused were Generics U.K. Ltd., Kent Pharmaceuticals Ltd., Regent-GM Laboratories Ltd., the Gold Shield Group Plc., Norton Healthcare Ltd., and Ranbaxy U.K. Ltd.
The SFO accused the drug companies of conspiring to defraud the NHS through a price fixing cartel.

Unfortunately for the SFO the case was thrown out of court on a technicality by Lord Justice Pritchard leaving an eight year investigation in tatters. The reason that the case failed was that the indictment by the

SFO was for price-fixing and price-fixing in itself is not a criminal offence. This defeat in a Court of Law has also has caused speculation as to the future of this Government body.

The case was a very expensive one but all is not lost fortunately as the NHS has managed to recoup £34 million from the drug companies with the assistance of the Department of Health with civil as opposed to criminal proceedings. The civil proceedings were simple because the drug firms did not have a case and could settle without accepting liability. It is rather touchingly poignant that the operation was probably named after a "portrait of a gentleman" by the artist Hans Holbein that hangs on the wall of the office of the SFO deputy chairman. If only there were more true gentlemen in the unscrupulous world of business!

The SFO were right to attempt to bring criminal proceedings against these powerful companies that were attempting to milk the NHS of billions of pounds with the price-fixing of drugs. These included Warfarin that is used to thin the blood in those with thrombosis. Altogether at least thirty drugs were involved at great expense to the struggling NHS. Although the SFO was unsuccessful in this case it seems that harsh criticism of this taskforce by journals such as The Lawyer is unmerited.

Ponzi Schemes:

The SFO has a long list of successful prosecutions to its credit. These include the sentencing in 2008 of five men involved in a ten billion US dollar worldwide Ponzi scheme. Two of the men were former British policemen and one was even a lawyer! The fraudsters were selling gold shares, a commodity, that had did not exist and had not even been mined.

Ponzi schemes are fraudulent investment scams that pay the investors dividends using other investors` money rather than from the profits of the actual business venture itself. In effect they are robbing Peter to pay Paul. In some cases there is not even a genuine business venture and the whole edifice is as flimsy as a pack of cards. It is difficult to comprehend that there are so many criminals, such as Bernie Madoff, that are willing to perpetrate such scams upon naïve and trusting investors.

Drug Companies:

The lucrative returns of pharmaceuticals make them an attractive target for counterfeit by organised powerful crime groups. These are medicines that are deliberately and fraudulently mislabelled as to their identity and their source. Use of such products can result in treatment failure and death. Both branded products and generic drugs are exposed to counterfeiting and may have identical packaging to the genuine product complete with the hologram. This level of sophistication can make detection difficult.

They may deceive health professionals, pharmacists and hospitals. These counterfeit drugs may contain some or no active ingredients. They are found all over the world and eliminating them presents a huge public health challenge. It is often impossible to trace the source of these dubious products. Counterfeiters are extremely flexible in the methods they use and may repeatedly change their methods to prevent detection. This means that there is a paucity of data as to the real extent of the problem.

The WHO estimates that one in ten of all medicines taken may be counterfeit. However the extent of the problem is disputed by statisticians and may be higher or lower
Some of the detected counterfeit drugs detected to date are Viagra for erectile dysfunction, Xenical for obesity, Zyprexa for bi-polar disorder, Lipitor to lower cholesterol, Metakelfin for malaria and numerous painkillers and over-the-counter products.

A deadly counterfeit diabetes drug containing six times the requisite dose resulted in several deaths in China recently. The U.K was flooded with counterfeit drugs in 2007 and this led to the eventual arrest of Kevin Xu, a citizen of the people `s republic of China and head of a large

counterfeiting enterprise. The MHRA seized 40 000 of the estimated 70 000 fake products and the rest were lost in the supply chain.
The medicines involved were those used to treat prostate cancer, schizophrenia and stroke.
The legislation to deal with his problem is the Offences under the Medicines Act 1968 and the Trademarks Act 1990. The maximum sentence under the former is two years and under the latter the maximum sentence is ten years. The MHRA prefers to prosecute under the Trademarks Act for this reason. However this is not always easy as the purpose of this Act is to protect the intellectual property rights of the company rather than protect the safety of the consumer. Counterfeit medicines tested by the Medicines and Healthcare products Regulatory Agency (MHRA) have been found to contain rat droppings and brick dust according to their head of enforcement Mr. Deats .

The vast profits to be made from pharmaceuticals encourage sharp business practice. Great caution is needed when appraisal is made of pharmaceutical companies such as AstraZenica, Allergan, Merck, GlaxoSmithKline, Pfizer and the hundreds of other brand names. Indeed a cursory glance at the very lengthy list of worldwide pharmaceutical companies will reveal that there must be a huge market for their wares. In the annual Fortune 500 survey the pharmaceutical industry has regularly made an appearance. Sharp business practice is routinely employed by these pharmaceutical giants.

In December the premises of Astrazenica were raided by EU officials investigating collusion and price rigging. A series of co-ordinated raids on Astrazenica offices in Europe unfolded as competition officials swooped without warning. The probe centred on a heartburn medication known as Nexium. Astrazenica deny any violation of EU antitrust rules that prohibit restrictive business practices. If found guilty the companied involved will face a hefty fine. The EU suspects that they planned to delay the entry of a generic drug into the market place. Generic drugs are copycat versions of drugs that are manufactured once the original patent has expired.

This causes the original price to plummet. The EU believes that stalling tactics have been used to delay the entry of generic copies of medicines into the markets in clear violation of competition rules. The very important implication of this sharp business practice is that health authorities such as the NHS lose billions of pounds a year as generic copycat versions are usually much cheaper. The makers of well known heartburn remedy Gaviscon, Reckitt Benckiser, were recently fined ten million pounds for over-charging the NHS. Clearly it is in the interests of pharmaceutical companies to behave themselves as such scandals invariably lead to a fall in the share prices.

The Serious Fraud office seized more than a million computer drives and files from the homes and offices of the companies involved . The police arrived with search warrants for six pharmaceutical companies but no arrests were made. The six companies accused were Generics U.K. Ltd., Kent Pharmaceuticals Ltd., Regent-GM Laboratories Ltd., the Gold Shield Group Plc., Norton Healthcare Ltd., and Ranbaxy U.K. Ltd. The SFO accused the drug companies of conspiring to defraud the NHS through a price fixing cartel. Unfortunately for the SFO the case was thrown out of court on a technicality by Lord Justice Pritchard leaving an eight year investigation in tatters.

The reason that the case failed was that the indictment by the SFO was for price-fixing and price-fixing in itself is not a criminal offence. This defeat in a Court of Law has also has caused speculation as to the future of this Government body. The case was a very expensive one but all is not lost a fortunately the NHS has managed to recoup £34 million from the drug companies with the assistance of the Department of Health with civil as opposed to criminal proceedings. The civil proceedings were simple because the drug firms did not have a case and could settle without accepting liability.

It is rather touchingly poignant that the operation was probably named after a “portrait of a gentleman” by the artist Hans Holbein that hangs on the wall of the office of the SFO deputy chairman. If only there were more true gentlemen in the unscrupulous world of business. The SFO were right to attempt to bring criminal proceedings against these ruthless companies that were attempting to milk the NHS of billions of pounds with the price-fixing of drugs such as Warfarin that is used to thin the blood in those with thrombosis.

Statins have been hailed as the wonder drug of our time and their promotion has been colossal. They are now taken by around seven million people in the United Kingdom and many are taking them as a prophylactic since they are in good health. A recent whole population study of Sweden with 4 million statin users showed no beneficial reduction in heart disease.

Statins like the cosmetic drug, Botox may weaken muscles. This can sometimes lead to muscle breakdown and a dangerous condition known as rhabddomyolosis. This condition can lead to kidney failure as the break down products block the delicate network of nephrous tubules. This dangerous condition has been especially linked to the cheaper statins such as Simvastatin. The National institute for Clinical Excellence (NICE) recommends the NHS to use cheaper statins. Researchers at St. George`s in the University of London have found that this cheaper statin does not protect as effectively against heart disease as the more expensive version named Atorvastatin. The cheaper statin is linked to rhabdomyolosis as well as type 2 diabetes.

Altogether at least thirty drugs were involved at great expense to the struggling NHS. Although the SFO was unsuccessful in this case it seems that harsh criticism of this taskforce by journals such as The Lawyer is unmerited.

The SFO has a long list of successful prosecutions to its credit. These include the sentencing in 2008 of five men involved in a ten billion US dollar worldwide Ponzi scheme. Two of the men were former British policemen and one was even a lawyer. The fraudsters were selling gold shares, a commodity, that had did not exist and had not even been mined.

Karl Marx felt that wealthy capitalists exploited the lower classes in order to remain at the top of the metaphorical pecking order. This exclusive situation is very much present in society today. Today many wealthy capitalists endeavour to do this by employing canny accountants to give advice on ways of avoiding paying taxes to the government. Numerous tax havens exist such as the Cayman Islands and this has recently received a lot of media attention in the light of austerity budgets. Ordinary hard working tax payers are becoming increasingly angry about flagrant tax avoidance.

There is a militant organisation called UK Uncut that protests against tax avoidance by companies such as Top shop. Rather embarrassingly for David Cameron, the boss of Top shop, Philip Green, was recently employed by him as an image consultant.
The wealthy donor to the Conservative Party, Lord Ashcroft, was also exposed as hiding all of his assets offshore.

The fact that he donated huge amounts to the election campaign is especially galling. Furthermore a recent report by the respected Institute of Fiscal Studies has shown that the draconian austerity cuts are being disproportionately shouldered by the poorest sector of society. This is manifestly unjust and the electorate is becoming increasingly restless with governments as recent street demonstrations have shown.
The general public is also very disenchanted with the behaviour of avaricious bankers who have been rewarding themselves with huge bonuses despite the collapse of many banks through mismanagement. This behaviour is beyond the comprehension of most ordinary mortals who are having moral panics.

Bankers are Sociopaths:

The criminologist David Nelken said that the best way to rob a bank is to work in one. Several high profile banks have collapsed recently.

These include Northern Rock, which precipitated the first run on a bank for decades. In America at least twenty eight banks collapsed including Lehman Brothers in 2008.

What on earth is going on here one may ask? Many say that the bankers gave out too many NINJA loans in America, NINJA being the acronym for no income, jobs or assets. This was known as the sub prime loan crisis. There is no doubt that bankers have been behaving recklessly in order to earn their sales commissions. Indeed these days a bank manager is required to be a good salesperson rather than a conscientious accountant.

It was reported in the Wall Street Journal that 279 banks have collapsed since 2008. To add insult to injury greedy bankers such as Fred Goodwin have not only brought the Royal Bank of Scotland to the brink of destruction but have handsomely remunerated themselves with millions of pounds in bonuses. No wonder that he earned the nickname Fred the Shred! He was ridiculed and pilloried in the popular press for weeks.

This is not just a recent phenomenon as it happened in 1995 to Barings Bank in Singapore when Nick Leeson became carried away with his investment strategy. Maybe Leeson and the other bankers were impelled by youthful creative testosterone to act in this way.

It has been calculated by the National Audit Office that each and every family in this country will eventually pay in the region of forty thousand pounds for the bank bailout. Yet what do the shareholders now get for their unwilling investment? It appears they receive little in the way of gratitude from the rescued banks as they continue to reward themselves with huge bonuses while refusing to lend to small businesses.

Many bankers are exhibiting signs of anti social or sociopathic behaviour. They are in effect behaving like psychopaths or “snakes in suits” While many human beings behave in an altruistic manner there is a small sub group that appear to be motivated entirely by self interest (Hare 1993). The term psychopath was coined by Hervey Cleckley in his textbook which analysed the behaviour patterns of people without scruples or conscience.

Psychopaths are described as being endowed with superficial charm, glibness, supreme self confidence and self belief. They do not hesitate to walk over others to get what they want. The profile of a psychopath perfectly describes that of many greedy bankers. Attempts have been made to quantify the exact extent of such corporate crime in terms of financial costs. It is speculated that the professions with the greatest proportion of sociopaths includes the legal profession, financer, surgeons, the military and politicians!

The behaviour of corrupt financiers may also be explained in terms of Game Theory or the Prisoners Dilemma. Game Theory shows how mutual co-operation or altruism will benefit both parties moderately. However if *one person only* cheats then he may emerge as the supreme victor at the complete expense of the other non-cheating participant. This cheating behaviour might be more prevalent in those with few emotional ties or bonds to a community.

This has led some social scientists to speculate that there may be an evolutionary niche for such selfish behaviour. In others words successful psychopaths may have evolved in society via a process of natural selection and so we see them everywhere today in the guise of rich bankers, politicians and businessmen. A check list has been designed to detect these traits that include lack of empathy, callousness and supreme narcissism . Maybe would be bankers should be made to take the PCL test to ascertain latent psychopathic tendencies?

Organised Crime:

In July 2010 Metropolitan Chief, Sir Paul Stephenson gave a lecture on organised crime groups at the John Harris Memorial lecture in London.

The boss of Scotland Yard said that were as many as six thousand criminal groups currently under the police radar. However this list of suspects does not include the greedy bankers who have fleeced the country of billions of pounds with their reckless investments and huge bonuses! Needless to say the majority of well organised criminals seldom see the inside of a prison. They are more likely to be found sunning themselves on a luxury yacht!

The types of crime under the police radar include drugs smuggling, people trafficking, financial fraud and counterfeiting. Clearly the numbers game is being won by the all omnipotent crime syndicates. No wonder that the police are waging an impossible battle with this invisible type of crime. It is far easier for a police officer to wage war on the motorist than it is delve into complicated and arcane crime labyrinths. Sir Paul said that there was no nationally co-ordinated means of tackling organised crime and he believed their activities cost the economy about forty billion pounds annually.

The Mob!

Well no one can argue that the Mafia is saintly! However these days most Mafiosi groups simply define themselves as astute businessmen who are not so very different from bankers in terms of shady financial deals and money laundering!

The Mafia earns ten per cent of the Gross Domestic Product ,or GDP. in Italy according to Confesercenti. These are worrying crime figures but caution is clearly required when bandying statistics around in this manner. This sum of forty billion pounds may be compared to the sum of seven billion pounds that Barclays Bank pays out in yearly bonuses! Clearly bankers and mobsters are not so very different!

When corporate malpractice or organised crime activities impinge on our health and safety then immediate action and prompt action is required.

Many consumer rackets such as adulterants in wine are due to organised crime groups.

The level of sophistry in organised crime groups as well as legitimate businesses is so high that one has to question whether any task force is capable of eradicating the corruption.

Organised crime wears many respectable guises. It is often not at all obvious who these criminals are as they have mastered the art of clever camouflage and blending in with the business environment. These invisible yet dangerous corporate criminals are all around us and in the most unexpected places. The really clever, successful ones make friends with people in high places and positions of power. They move seamlessly in high society. They achieve positions of trust and are beyond suspicion. It is usually their minions further down the hierarchical ladder who are invariably caught. The gargantuan profits of their racketeering are cleanly laundered into respectable business ventures such as hotels, restaurants, property and charitable trusts.

Disorganised Crime Attracts Attention!

It is the "disorganised" as opposed to the "organised" crime outfits that tend to attract unwanted attention. The endless killings and feuds between the Mexican cartels is a classic example of serious "disorganised" crime.

Thousands of drug related murders have taken place in Mexico during one of the bloodiest decades in the country `s history. Recently Mexican police found the bodies of fourteen decapitated bodies in a shopping centre in Acapulco. They were believed to have been murdered for trying to intrude on a rival gang `s turf or patch.

Acapulco has become the focus of fierce and bloody battles between rival cartels with many gruesome murders. This dramatic rise in violence has seriously damaged the reputation and tourist prospects of Acapulco. At least fifty thousand people have been killed in drug related violence in Mexico. A President, named Felipe Calderon once launched an offensive against the drug cartels. Clearly this is not having a desired or beneficial outcome. Many murders have taken place in broad daylight and in front of tourists.

In contrast well organised crime manages to operate with the absolute minimum of violence. For example most countries are awash with heroin and other recreational drugs, yet the streets are not littered with corpses as in Mexico! Clearly this non violent situation is infinitely preferable to one where turf related murder is commonplace. The well organised mob model shows how a sophisticated outfit can trade without drawing unwarranted attention although there have been a lot of heroin drug overdoses. This is not to condone their activities known as "business" , but the situation is clearly preferable to the chaos currently erupting in Mexico.

A lot of revenue is produced and often this is ploughed back into the community. Money may be laundered or reinvested back into community concerns such as restaurants and shops, even educational charities, that contribute greatly to a city` s vibrancy and diversity. In these tough economic times many small businesses are closing in the face of severe financial constraints.

This has led to a sorry situation where many streets are full of boarded up shops. In some cities a quarter of the smaller shops are now boarded up. Conversely, small businesses that are helped or part funded by crime syndicates are able to continue trading in times of recession and austerity. This brings life, colour and prosperity to the streets. Also the City Council receives revenue from such traders in the form of business rates. It is not ideal but certainly preferable to the violent scenario in Mexico.

This conundrum depicts that there are no simple black and white answers to this issue, merely subtle shades of grey. It may be the case that such sophisticated groups should be left well alone if they endeavour to peacefully co exist within a community. The history of mankind indicates that people will always want to dabble with mind altering substances. Therefore it is probably futile and inadvisable to attempt to stamp out the narcotics trade.

Often police intervention can seriously disrupt the harmony of well organised groups. Such intervention may lead to internal repercussions as accusations of "grassing" erupt within the group. These recriminations could lead to violence. This would cause the well organised operation to become disorganised. Sometimes the police chiefs have a little arrangement going that will prevent such scenarios! The sanctity of human life should always be paramount in good policing! Therefore a government backed war on drugs is probably ill advised.

Corporate Criminals evade detection:

One has to look at this in the context of how much of taxpayers` money is also being wasted by legitimate authorities who are running our economy such as elected politicians and financial institutions. These institutions have defrauded the taxpayer of considerable sums in a way that mimics the operations of organised crime groups.

No wonder then that the average police officer prefers to target motoring crime!

SOCA was crime busting outfit was created by the Labour Government to deal with sophisticated crime. The agency was criticised by the Conservatives for only managing to recover £78 million from the proceeds of crime in three years. The cost of running the agency was put at £1.2 billion meaning that the operation was running at a loss to the taxpayer. In July 2010 there was a trumpeted fanfare of massive reform and overhaul of SOCA to be replaced by the NCA or National Crime Agency.

This acronym is nowhere near as sexy or as memorable as the acronym SOCA. It seems that each time a new political Party takes the reins of power they feel the need to put their own individual political stamp on the country.

The coalition are hoping to introduce radical changes in the Police Force with the introduction of elected Police Commissioners. The theory behind this startling innovation is that those elected by the public would be more accountable to them. Needless to say all this political tinkering

with policing has not gone down well with the Association of Chief Police Officers commonly designated as ACPO.
This police company is also to be stripped of its power to run undercover units following recent controversies about its Ratcliffe on Stour operation. Embarrassed Police Minister Nick Herbert has announced that ACPO is to be stripped of all operational duties following the risible antics of undercover officers.

Undercover officers employed to infiltrate activist groups ended up being the main protagonists and perpetrators of the acts of sabotage. This resulted in the police National Public Order Unit becoming an object of hilarity and ridicule. Certainly in January 2011 the press had a field day devoting several pages to the salacious, seedy exploits of the hapless police officer Mark Kennedy, who now says that he lives in fear of his life.

The National Public Order Unit costs five million pounds a year to run. It was set up initially to infiltrate animal rights groups who had sent letter bombs in the 1990`s. The Unit appears to have lost its way. The secretive Unit has now received such a blare of publicity one has to wonder about its future operational success. It seems that all the organisations which are attempting to uphold law and order are currently falling into disrepute. It is small wonder then that so many powerful crime groups are evading capture or detection and driving Sir Paul Stephenson to despair.

The police have also come under fire for using the controversial kettling technique of crowd control. The premise of kettling is to prevent the crowd running riot and causing mayhem and criminal damage. However the technique has a serious drawback in that it indiscriminately herds up large numbers of innocent passersby. In 1989 bad policing of crowds led to the Hillsborough disaster where many football fans were crushed to death.

Police tactics :

Recently the technique of kettling was used during the student riots and this led to many complaints and threats of lawsuits. Innocent tourists as well as legitimate student protesters were kettled for several hours without food, drink or access to bathrooms. Some people fainted and many were hypothermic as the day turned to night. Some young school children started to burn their school books in an effort to keep warm. This was maliciously interpreted as acts of vandalism.
However the poor children interviewed were clearly cold, hungry and frightened.
This incident portrays the abuses of those holding the reins of power. These are certainly crimes against humanity. It depicts the abuse of Government State power as well as police powers of unlawful detainment. The angry Home Secretary even spoke of using water cannon against the crowd. Imagine the distress that would have caused to the already freezing cold hypothermic children.

The police have also attacked innocent bystanders without provocation. Ian Tomlinson was killed by an unprovoked blow to his back as he walked passed a row of policemen at the G20 protests in London.
The police have also used pepper spray that has resulted in deaths. The peaceful anti racist protester Blair Peach was bludgeoned to death by a police baton in 1979.

The weaponry of the police is becoming more suited to Armed Forces personnel. The police now use tasers and other supposedly less lethal weapons. A new long range acoustic device (LRAD) was used in Philadelphia University on peaceful students and lecturers. This ultrasonic device causes excruciating pain in the ear as well as disorientation and collapse. It may even lead to deafness! Here in England the mosquito device has been used in South Wales and an Oxford shopping precinct to deter young people from loitering.

The Mosquito emits a painful ultrasound noise that can only be heard by young adults and children. It has been rightly criticised by human rights groups such as Liberty and Amnesty. The police have also abused the stop and search powers of the anti terrorism Acts to target and harass ethnic minorities. In 1981 the hated SUS Laws gave rise to the Brixton and Toxteth riots. Plainly most of those stopped and searched are not terrorists.

There is plenty of evidence to suggest that minority groups have been unfairly discriminated against by police use of Stop and Search Laws says the Ministry of Justice. Indeed following the Lawrence inquiry the police were branded as being "institutionally racist". Institutional racism was a term first coined by Sir William MacPherson following police failures in the investigation of the tragic death of Stephen Lawrence. It referred to a collective failure to provide an appropriate service to people because of their ethnicity.

The Director General of Prisons Martin Narey warned that the prison service is institutionally racist and proportionately more BME groups have died in custody. It has also been estimated that BME groups are up to eight times more likely to be stopped and searched by the police using anti terror legislation. Indeed the Archbishop John Sentamu, who is from Uganda, complained that he himself has been stopped and searched several times when wearing secular clothing. Dr. John Sentamu believes that he has been stopped by police purely because of his Ugandan heritage. Under section 44 of the Anti Terrorism Act 2000 the police can stop and search anyone in a designated place on the merest hint of a suspicion. Any person the police might not like the look of may be searched under the pretext of national security. This has led to flagrant abuse of the powers by police officers.

Every year there are around 150 thousand searches carried out by over zealous police officers in great Britain. This unacceptable police behaviour contravenes the Race Relations Act of 1974 which was amended in 2003. Tourists innocently taking photographs of iconic buildings such as the London Eye fell foul of the draconian legislation and many ethnic minorities were harassed. This led to widespread complaints by civil liberty groups such as Liberty. Following a test case by a complainant a judicial precedent was set. Henceforth the European Court of Human Rights ruled that the powers of stop and search were being abused and therefore deemed illegal.

The powers of the State have come under a lot of scrutiny recently. Civil liberties groups are concerned at the gradual intrusion of the State into their personal lives. There are countless CCTV cameras for each citizen in the U.K. and the Orwellian predictions of 1984 have well and truly arrived. Each of us is approximately caught on camera one thousand times a week! A school was criticised for having no fewer than one hundred cameras trained on its pupils. One million innocent people have had their DNA placed on a National Database against their wishes. Local Authorities have spied on blameless households using RIPA terrorist legislation looking for such heinous crimes as those relating to school catchment areas or parking misdemeanours.

There was a public outcry at David Blunkett` s idea of ID cards which have now been shelved. However the use of biometric devices is increasing and even used in schools to check attendance via fingerprinting children as they arrive. This is wholly unacceptable and I complained about this treatment of learners in my role as School Governor. Recently a Protection of Freedoms Bill has been proposed by the coalition to try and counter this incipient erosion of freedoms by the all powerful and watchful State. It is also rather ironic that politicians who make the laws have been recently exposed as breaking the laws with their expenses!

It seems that any person in a position of power may be tempted to abuse this power. This is the case in unseen crimes such as domestic violence which is seldom reported to the police. There is often a lot of stigma attached to being bullied and the victim might feel ashamed. This idea of shame is summed up in the excellent title of a book by domestic violence campaigner, Erin Pizzey called “scream quietly or the neighbours might hear”. Women may also be harassed sexually and even sexually assaulted by their partners or beaten brutally. The strong in any society often seek to dominate the weak.

It is often the case that those in a position of power or authority may be tempted to abuse their position. This finding was demonstrated by the infamous Stanford Prison experiment conducted in Stanford University. Half of the students were dressed as prisoners and half as prison guards. The pretend student prison guards behaved in such a bullying manner to the fake prisoners that the experiment had to be halted as the students started to show signs of a break down. People are easily corrupted by power and this has important implications for the weak and vulnerable in our society.

It appears that the urge for financial gain, status and hierarchical advantage motivates much of human behaviour and this may lead to transgressions of the prevailing laws in the particular jurisdiction.
Human beings evolved to compete for scarce food resources and territory via survival of the fittest. Therefore these competitive instincts need to be kept under control.
The hunting instincts of prehistoric man may be compared to the dangerous and competitive urges in modern man. These competitive urges may motivate status driven, acquisitive crime and power related crimes. Like a prehistoric hunter modern man may metaphorically "go for the kill" to seal a business deal. Often powerful groups or individuals get away with their wrongdoings.
As the well known criminological saying goes, the rich get richer and the poor get prison !

Chapter Two: Equality and Diversity

The twenty first century has certainly been legislatively active regarding equality and diversity. This is, in part thanks to the efforts of Labour Minister Harriet Harman. That everyone, regardless of gender, race, age or creed, should be treated with fairness and respect is an accepted truism of our times. These principles have been enshrined in the 2010 Equality Act. Therefore one would hope that the probation service will embrace the prevailing zeitgeist by providing a service worthy of our current legislature.

In other words, it should aim to do justice to diversity and difference and the subject of this essay will now be explored.
Let us ask ourselves the question "what does the term "difference" imply? The word implies that certain groups are different from the norm. In other words women, older citizens and ethnic minorities are deemed to be sufficiently different from the norm as to require legislative protection from discrimination by it. The norm is presumably epitomised by a white male patriarchy. Is this white male patriarchy omnipresent in our judicial system? Yes, indeed there is evidence to indicate that our judicial courts of law are replete with Justices from a comfortable background of privilege and wealth, and predominantly of the white male genre.

This realisation has propelled some criminologists along an investigatory path to ascertain whether minorities are receiving a fair trial or in the case of women a courtly chivalrous trial. Indeed the question of how the entire criminal justice system treats women and minority groups is a large and possibly vexatious one.
The enigmatic judicial logic of the Magistrates court sometimes sentences defendants as flawed women rather than as lawbreaking citizens . A wealth of literature describes this judicial bias against women.

Magistrates are often swayed by the prevailing sentencing culture of the bench. In other words the sentences they mete out may be the result of whim and whimsy and do not uphold the principles of justice. This inherent bias may result in harsher sentences meted out to those from a less privileged back ground than the Magistrates or Judge. Women who transgress unrealistically high societal expectations may be labelled as doubly deviant wicked women in need of reform . Yet women tend to commit far fewer crimes than men in every field except for prostitution, the latter offence often driven by financial hardship.

The question of how the probation service should apply just and fair practice will be examined within the entire judicial framework. This judicial framework encompasses the courts, the police, the prisons and above all the probation service.

The Equality Act ensures that each and every one of us has a right to receive fair, impartial and neutral treatment. This premise of equality should be ubiquitous in the criminal justice system. Yet there are indications to the contrary. Women are often sentenced according to a judicial logic that sees them as fallen women rather than as perpetrators of minor offences. In Victorian England women who misbehaved were seen as needing moral protection In Italy women may be either placed on a pedestal as a Madonna Virgin Mary, or are considered to be unworthy sinful women. This simplistic black or white thinking is a form of prejudice via stereotyping.

Human beings seem to be easily seduced by such facile thinking which requires little cognitive effort. It may be the case that people are fundamentally inclined towards an oversimplification of their environment. The desire to file everything and everyone in neat compartments or categories may appeal to an inherent sense of tidy order. However, it is precisely this kind of behaviour that inadvertently results in narrow minded thinking and prejudice. The word prejudice itself comes from the Latin word meaning to pre judge. In other words a judgement has already been made that has no foundation on the facts of the case or the person.

Numerous studies have shown how easy it is to be seduced by such lazy thinking. This tendency to label others as outsiders may result from any perceived difference to the self referenced “norm”. Once a person has been labelled as an outsider, it then becomes easier to see them as worthy of punishment within the criminal justice system. The labelling of perceived socially deviant non conformists has been discussed by numerous sociologists.

The danger of such labelling is that those who are labelled may become deviant via the process of a self fulfilling prophecy (Merton 1995). Studies have shown how perceived expectations of behaviour may result in the actual behaviour occurring. For instance, if a teacher has positive expectations of a pupil, then that learner may indeed go on to achieve better than average results. Conversely if a teacher has negative expectations then the learner may under achieve in their school work. It is clear to see then, why negative expectations of a labelled subgroup may result in actual negative behaviour by that prejudged group. This is the self fulfilling prophecy in action. Those in a position of hierarchical power may find that it suits them to label as deviant those that may disrupt their status quo.

For example back in the swinging sixties the Conservative politician Enoch Powell made disparaging comments about "hippies". The straight laced politician may have felt the long haired freaks presented a threat to his status quo with their free and open ideologies. Even worse was to come in 1968 with the infamous "rivers of blood" speech which aimed to incite racial hatred against immigrants. Enoch Powell delivered an impassioned speech warning that terrible dangers to the community would result and blood would flow in the streets, if immigration continued unchecked.

He was exhibiting a classic behaviour pattern of stereotyping groups of people into neat compartments. However each and every person is a unique and diverse individual. Therefore it is unwise to allot whole groups of people into a particular category. Indeed there is now legislation to ensure that this does not happen in this country.
The situation is not so benign in other countries where a man may be executed for practising homosexuality.

Today the new buzz words are equality and diversity. However the old ingrained habits of some reactionaries are hard to change as the recent spate of workplace litigation has shown. Employees have successfully sued for sexist comments. Some critics feel that the pendulum of political correctness may have swung a little too far in the other direction. This is illustrated by the recent case of a bottom slapping woman taken to court. The lady was reported for sexual harassment after allegedly patting a male colleague` s derriere in a friendly manner! This time the law lords decided that enough was enough and threw the vexatious case out of court.

There is no room for complacency however as statistics reveal that latent discrimination still runs deep within the criminal justice system. For instance, the rates of incarceration for women in this country appear to be rising dramatically. This finding indicates that alternatives to custodial sentences are not being sufficiently used within the criminal justice system and that women are being unfairly sentenced. Sometimes magistrates may be reluctant to fine Mothers of children as they feel that they are taking the food from the mouths of hungry children.

They may equally feel that hard physical unpaid work is unsuitable for the delicate feminine physique and may prevent a mother from caring for her child. Perversely and illogically this thinking may sometimes result in a custodial sentence being imposed!

Clearly the best solution would be to use a probation order that is tailored to the needs of a woman with children. Such an order would ideally be implemented to advise, assist and befriend the troubled offender. Many community orders are designed with the male offender population in mind and this fact should not surprise us since most offenders are indeed male. Statistics show that women commit substantially fewer crimes than men. Therefore there is a cogent argument for the closure of women` s prisons in line with the Corston Report .

Jean Corston calls for a holistic woman centred approach that provides support for women offenders rather than punishment. She believes that most women offenders are in need of guidance rather than further punishment. Many women may be driven to offend as a result of long term abuse or domestic violence.
Sometimes women are criminalised for poverty as when they are sent to prison for being unable to pay fines.
Often women are driven to offend by financial need. An example of this is when a woman prostitute is fined by a court for soliciting and she has no money with which to pay the fine. She therefore goes back out to work on the streets to earn the money to pay the court imposed fine. Thus a vicious cycle of reoffending is perpetuated by poverty. Such need driven offending is often in stark contrast to the masculine "doing gender" male offending behaviour. The "Saturday night is great for a fight" type of offending committed by testosterone fuelled men is in stark contrast to much of women` s offending .

In contrast many women may offend out of necessity rather than for the thrill of it. Sometimes they fall victim to male coercion as in the case of perjury where a woman is persuaded to cover up for a boyfriend or husband. Some men undoubtedly enjoy a good brawl but most women are unhappy while offending. The Corston Report indicates that many women sent to prison have come from a background of deprivation and may have been brought up in care homes. Many have a substance problem indicating that they have become prey of exploitative drug dealers. The report emphasised the mental health fragility of many women offenders.

Sometimes women are trafficked by organised crime gangs to work as prostitutes. Therefore it would seem unjust to further punish these women by sending them to prison. The Corston Report highlighted the mental health fragility of many women offenders who may self harm in stressful environments such as prison. Clearly most women offenders are in need of support and this should be reflected in the probations service provided. Many of their offences pale into significance when compared with the corporate crimes of white collar criminals . Perpetrators of white collar crime may embezzle millions or even put lives at risk via negligence and escape censure. In contrast a woman may be dealt with harshly for being unable to pay for a television licence.

The aforementioned reasons make for a pressing case to adopt a soft touch approach when dealing with women offending. The most humane approach would be to use an "advise, assist, befriend" probation order as typified by John Augustus in days gone by. The one to one casework model is preferable for vulnerable minorities as it provides continuity of care and caring interpersonal relations. It would help teach good behaviour via pro social modelling (PSM) and positive reinforcement. Sadly this style of probation is currently on the wane. Nowadays offenders are managed rather than befriended. They are quantified as parcels of risk to the insecure public and such dehumanisation may worsen their plight. What would the pioneering founder of probation, John Augustus think of this turn of events one may wonder? The "one to one" relationship between the probation officer and the offender is gradually receding into the archives of oblivion and a mire of bureaucracy.

This clearly is not a satisfactory situation. Instead of a friendly personal rapport with the probation officer an offender now has to deal with an impersonal cohort of officials. This managerialism will depersonalise the offender who now has become a package of risk rather than a person in need of assistance. It also might reduce job satisfaction for the service provider. The human interface is gradually disappearing under a mountain of paperwork and form filling. This cannot be satisfactory and indeed the outcome of such an approach may lead to defiance. A person in need of help may be passed around the various departments as in the game of pass the parcel. This is a real person` s life and should not be treated as a party game.

The emphasis today is insidiously shifting to one of quantifying risk to the public. A points system is used to quantify such risk ranging from a low number to a high number. There is even a misguided sense of status in the practitioners overseeing the higher risk numbers in their charge. Probation has become a numbers game. This use of numbers evokes a disturbing parody of the cult series of the sixties "the Prisoner" starring Patrick McGoohan. The Prisoner has lost his identity and become just a number. Once a person becomes dehumanised in this way it becomes much easier to mistreat them. There are inherent dangers to this impersonal numerical approach that typifies the casework management model.

The statutory provision to protect the public may result in the client assuming a heavy burden of risk. In 1984 the Home Office introduced SNOP (Statement of National Operations and Purpose). The aim of SNOP is to make the probation service more accountable and to provide an evidence base. This was followed by the introduction of the National Probation Service in 2001.The government understandably wants value for money.

In the case management probation model the service may be fragmented and disjointed because of the multi agency approach. The detached case manager giving orders from his lofty ivory tower may make mistakes regarding a client that he has little rapport with. The offender may be treated more harshly as a result and this will not facilitate rehabilitation.
There is the possibility that women or minority groups might be placed in a higher risk group by mistake. This could occur because of latent prejudice. A form of uptariffing could occur within the probation service whereby a BME client is placed in a higher risk group than is warranted by the actual offence. This uptariffing of risk might occur for example if the client is deemed to come from an impoverished background.

Furthermore, is it wise to make extrapolations to minority groups from research that has been conducted predominantly on white male majority groups? This question has been widely considered. There is a growing consensus that more research is needed on what works for women.

Women may find it hard to comply with community orders, especially if they have children.

They might then be labelled as being non compliant and further punished. One must always bear in mind that their crimes may have been constructed as such by a patriarchal and censorious society. These women may not be paragons of virtue but they may not merit the description of criminal either. A label of criminal may be used to assert the hegemony of the dominant ruling tier.
Law may be seen as the normative structure of the dominant group that will always treat minorities harshly. Those in a position of power will be able to transform their cultural norms into laws of the land. This will inevitably result in the minorities being unfairly discriminated against.

Therefore it is wise to build up a trusting relationship with the client from a minority group who may have already lost faith in human nature. By establishing a warm and trusting relationship, the client may learn new pro social skills. This may be the first time that the client has ever encountered such positive pro social behaviour. It may lead to a moment of self discovery. These new pro social skills will eventually enable the client to improve his or her behaviour in the future.

There is a great opportunity to affect a change in a person` s life choices by teaching pro social skills via setting a good example. This is not a difficult option to implement. A meta-analysis showed that a humane client focussed service is “what works” best for women. All that is required is for the probation officer to act with kindness and to show good manners towards the client. This approach will provide legitimacy in the client relationship. Since the probation officer is now perceived to be a legitimate source of authority there is a greater likelihood of compliance.

Therefore there really is no place for penal retributivism in the rehabilitation of offenders. This may seem an unpalatable truth to many in the grip of moral panics. Yet it should be obvious that to turn the other cheek is preferable to the dictum an eye for an eye and a tooth for a tooth. Punishing a person will result in anger that may lead to extralegal behaviour and defiance. In other words more law breaking!!

Penal populism may appeal to the insecure electorate but does the electorate really know what is good for itself? The revolving door of recidivism demonstrates that harsh punishment is not the solution to cure antisocial behaviour. Perhaps a gentler approach will yield better results. It does not always take a sledgehammer to crack a nut. Providing a supportive shoulder to lean upon may lead to a renewed trust in humanity. With this renewed trust in mankind may come new hope that the world is not such a harsh and uncaring place filled with malign authoritarian figures.

This realisation may lead to a reintegration back into society. An integrated member will then be likely to feel a sense of shame in future when doing wrong .This uncomfortable sensation of mortification may persuade the client that it is better to conform to societal norms. This is because he or she now feels a warm sense of "attached, involved, and committed belief in society". This client centred approach embraces the ideals of John Augustus and those who followed his footsteps.

These days the orthodox approach to probation has been superseded by a revisionist approach that may be drifting away from the original doctrine to "advise, assist and befriend". The early revisionists felt that offenders were moral degenerates whose souls needed to be saved from eternal damnation and hellfire. Even worse there was the Edwardian idea of the deserving and the undeserving poor implying that only a select few deserved assistance .Nevertheless much credit must be given to the Edwardians for the introduction of probation as an alternative to custodial sentencing in 1907.

This was the age of the Liberal reforming politicians such as Asquith and maverick David Lloyd George, who was nicknamed "Merlin the Welsh Wizard" for his ingenuity and charisma. This radical Liberal set out to improve the lives of the poor and oppressed and became known as the people` s champion. My very own beloved ancestor David Lloyd George, was a free unconventional spirit who bent the rules to get his radical reforms such as the Peoples `Budget, passed through Parliament and the House of Lords. Thus the Probation Act of 1907 became law to befriend and assist the oppressed. Other radical reforming philanthropists include Elizabeth Fry and John Howard, the namesake of the present day Howard League of Penal Reform.

These days there is a tendency to see a probation order in a more punitive light. Since 1991 probation has become a sentence in its own right. The Inspectorate HMIP proposed a new slogan for probation in 2006.The zeitgeist is to "punish, help, change and control". The early humanitarian ideals of John Augustus are slowly being usurped by the impersonal mechanics of public sector managerialism. Since 1995 the caring social work component of probation seems to be insidiously retreating into the mists of time.

In 1993 Michael Howard enthused that "prison works". However the premise of this book is to question the assertion that prison works and that prison is the best option for offenders. For a start many of the most successful corporate and financial criminals often manage to evade detection altogether. Prisons may have a role to serve in protecting the public from a cohort of very dangerously violent criminals but on the whole such violent criminals are in the minority of offenders.

In 1997 came more forceful words such as "tough on crime, tough on the causes of crime" uttered by Tony Blair. Does this tough love approach work with women offenders or minority groups? There is evidence that what works for men does not necessarily work for women. This may be due to the fact that many community programmes are designed with men in mind. For example the OASIS programme was developed by a male ex offender. Therefore it may be biased towards the male perspective and not be suitable for women` s needs.

The client served by the probation service may feel that they have already suffered enough prior to being engulfed by the criminal justice system. This is especially likely to be the case with minority groups and women. There is plenty of evidence to suggest that minority groups have been unfairly discriminated against by police use of Stop and Search Laws . Indeed following the Lawrence inquiry the police were branded as being "institutionally racist".

Institutional racism was a term first coined by Sir William MacPherson following police failures in the investigation of the tragic death of Stephen Lawrence. It referred to a collective failure to provide an appropriate service to people because of their ethnicity .The Director General of Prisons Martin Narey warned that the prison service is institutionally racist in 2001 and proportionately more BME groups have died in custody .

It has also been estimated that BME groups are up to eight times more likely to be stopped and searched by the police using anti terror legislation. Indeed the Archbishop John Sentamu, who is from Uganda, complained that he himself has been stopped and searched several times when wearing secular clothing. Dr. John Sentamu believes that he has been stopped by police purely because of his Ugandan heritage.
Back in the 1970`s the over use of hated "SUS" laws led to the Brixton and Toxteth riots in 1981.

There is today a growing consensus that the anti terror legislation is still being abused by the police to target ethnic minorities. Under section 44 of the Anti Terrorism Act 2000 the police can stop and search anyone in a designated place on the merest hint of a suspicion. Any person the police might not like the look of may be searched under the pretext of national security. This has led to flagrant abuse of the powers by police officers.

In a single year there are around 150 thousand searches carried out by over zealous police officers . Tourists innocently taking photographs of iconic buildings such as the London Eye fell foul of the draconian legislation and many ethnic minorities were harassed. This led to widespread complaints by civil liberty groups such as Liberty. Following a test case by a complainant in 2010, a judicial precedent was set. Henceforth the European Court of Human Rights ruled that the powers of stop and search were being abused and therefore deemed illegal.

It is clear then that the minority groups are disproportionately targeted by the criminal justice system and therefore may arrive in greater numbers in the probation service. Once inside the net of the probation service ethnic minorities may be placed into a higher risk category than their criminogenic needs actually warrant .

In other words they have been unjustly stereotyped. It seems profoundly unjust to impose a retributive order on an unfairly targeted and selected sample of the population. Such BME groups may already be nursing a profound sense of estrangement and grievance against the biased system that put them in such a position .

They may have been stopped purely on the basis of ethnicity and subsequently found to be in possession of class B drugs. Yet it is widely reported that there is a culture of cocaine use among bankers in London` s square mile who may be less likely to be stopped if they are white skinned. This police behaviour contravenes the Race Relations Act of 1974 which was amended in 2003.
Therefore many minority groups that have been apprehended may be nursing a sense of injustice that needs to be dealt with sensitively by the probation service. Since certain sectors of the criminal justice system have been shown to be institutionally racist it is incumbent upon the probation service to try and make amends. Thereby some sort of equitable redress may be provided to balance the scales of justice.

Is this the case today and does the probation service do justice for difference and diversity? This is a subject that warrants extensive investigation. Perhaps the focus could be shifted to examine the social milieu and cultural context in which the offending behaviour takes place .

This focus on the broader picture helps to contextualise and understand the individual client` s needs. The Probation Inspectorate has already considered the problems facing minority BME groups (Her Majesty` s Inspectorate of Probation) but there is always the danger that this area will be neglected. The relatively high percentage of foreign nationals in custody might indicate to us that the opportunity for a more lenient probation order has been passed over .

In 2006 a tragic racist murder occurred in Feltham Young Offenders` Institution that was facilitated by prison guards who had placed victim, Zahid Mubarak, in a cell with a violent racist. A Home Office report had previously indicated that prison staff in approved premises had not received sufficient anti racist training. The foreign national and BME groups do not have an organisation comparable to the Corston Independent Funders Coalition to help them. The Corston Independent Funders Coalition is a group of charities that aims to support women and divert them from custody.

In 2018 they announced £2 million for the women` s diversionary fund in collaboration with the Ministry of Justice. This funding will enable further provision of the one-stop shop services that help women with bail conditions and work with NOMS to find approved accommodation. The Women` s Centres Forum encompasses thirty eight diversionary projects for women in England and Wales. These diversionary community projects include one stop shops to assist women with substance abuse problems, domestic violence, homelessness and mental health problems. The Together Woman Project also founded one stop shops for women across Yorkshire to assist them with every stage of the criminal justice system.

In Bradford TWP runs alternative to custody orders. A high rate of compliance was found. This supportive and practical service is obviously "what works" with women. A cost benefit analysis showed great savings may be made using intensive support. It costs £2000 per year per person to run compared to the £40 000 a year for a prison place that may well drive a woman to self harm. It is important also to consider value for money in the probation service. The London Probation Service recently provoked an outcry when it sent an e-mail to Magistrates asking that they impose curfews instead of probation to save money!

A supportive and caring approach is clearly the way forward for vulnerable female offenders and may ultimately save money. The Revolving Doors is another charity that offers help for those with multiple problems who come in contact with the criminal justice system. The Time Out centre in Glasgow provides a lot of support to women addicts and aims to empower women.

The Home Office has introduced a joined up multi agency approach to assist women known by the acronym WORP (Women` s Offending Reduction Programme). It makes more sense to invest money in community projects that serve to empower women and boost their self esteem.

It does not benefit women to drag them into the net of a punitive criminal justice system. The probation service is currently functioning in an impersonal and bureaucratic way. This will cause emotional stress to those dragged into it especially vulnerable women and minority groups. The consequences of being dragged through the CJS are harmful and cause distress to dependent children. A non treatment paradigm approach has been discussed by criminologists.

Their approach is quintessentially based upon an edifice of respect for all people. Treat others as you would wish to be treated yourself. This is the basis for the non treatment paradigm. The aim of this gentle approach is to help with problems that have been identified by the client. Another approach believes in the efficacy of cognitive behavioural therapy which enhances basic reasoning skills.

This concept was invented by Aaron Beck who was influenced by behaviourists such as B.F. Skinner and his operant conditioning theories. Each of us can analyse our basic thinking patterns and try to reprogram destructive thoughts with Cognitive Behaviour Therapy. Reasoning and Rehabilitation (R&R) are thinking skills that help prevent recidivism and were first studied in Canada. Learning to stop and think before impulsive acts may help the client to break ingrained destructive patterns of behaviour. The conclusion is that there is still a lot of work to be done within the criminal justice system in order to comply with equality and diversity legislation.

The probation service needs to treat minority groups with special sensitivity and compassion as they may have arrived there through misfortune and unfair police targeting. The impersonal managerialism of the service may alienate the client and result in non compliance. Therefore a supportive "one to one relationship" teaching pro social skills is preferable to the risk oriented management model. Women also benefit from community projects such as Evolve that serve to empower them. In these times of budget cuts it would be a great shame if the Home Office withdrew funding from such progressive community schemes.

Chapter Three: Are Womens` Prisons, a good idea?

This chapter will examine the ideal that women` s prisons should be abolished in England in line with the recommendation of the Corston Report and will provide critical arguments for this closure.
There are fourteen women` s prisons in England and none in Wales; some prisons for men also accept women.

Immediately one can envisage that if all the women prisons were to be closed in line with the wishes of Baroness Corston and The Howard League for Penal Reform, women may end up inside men` s prisons in a law of unintended consequences.

Therefore although the principle of abolishing such prisons is undoubtedly based upon sound humanitarian ideals, one has to be wary of embracing the idea with evangelical zeal. Let us now examine some of the many arguments for women` s prisons to be abolished in England .These include feminist theories of " malestream " gendered justice.

Currently there are 4,341 female prisoners in England (H. M. Prison Service 2010) many of whom are vulnerable foreign nationals, drug dependant and fragile. This number can be compared to the 64 thousand women in Russian prisons many for minor offences .There are proportionately more women on remand than men. Many are later freed after trial supporting our argument for prison closure.

There is a greater risk of self harm and suicide among women prisoners. They are more adversely affected by the intimidating prison architectural environment as most prisons were designed with men in mind. There is evidence that these women have been treated unfairly by the inherently patriarchal criminal justice system as over one third of these women have had no previous convictions. Furthermore an equal proportion of one third, have suffered domestic violence and in effect were already victims prior to incarceration.

Two thirds of these women also enter prison with a mental health and substance problem indicating that they had become prey of exploitative drug dealers. Many of these women come from a background of a deprived childhood having been brought up in care homes (Prison Reform Trust). In short, these women appear to come from a disadvantaged and lower echelon of society and in need of support rather than further punishment.

Women are sentenced while pregnant and a woman was shackled to the delivery bed in Styal Prison in 1993. Many women have dependant children and the pernicious effect of child separation needs to be considered. Although there are eight Mother and baby units, none of the units cater for infants older than eighteen months. One can imagine the extreme trauma that ensues when separation occurs at this age. Mothers and babies may have bonded and deep emotional attachments formed. To deprive an infant of his or her Mother at this age is deeply damaging according to psychological research.

These researchers and many others have demonstrated that such separations may cause a child to become withdrawn and lose trust in adults completely. The child may even become delinquent in the future as a result of such perceived abandonment. In short this enforced separation may result in irrevocable damage to the child who may become an offender as an adult, thus perpetuating a long term vicious cycle, through the generations.

Even if the child becomes a law abiding member of society, the hurt and pain will remain deeply embedded in the psyche causing long term depression, apathy or even a state known as “learned helplessness”.

This phenomenon was discovered by experiments where caged animals were subjected to unrelenting stress with no escape. They simply gave up trying to escape after a while. Later when an escape route *was in fact possible* they did not attempt to escape. They had in other words learned to be helpless and behaved in an apathetic manner. Much the same depressive behaviour has been seen in people who have become resigned to their situation and simply *give up*. This is typical of doleful reactions resulting from prison, as well as infant mother separations.

This suffering of children and women is a cogent argument for the closure of women`s prisons .Nearly a third of such children are taken into care and so may be permanently separated from their Mothers. One third of women prisoners lose their homes, and even their precious possessions while in prison, so are greatly disadvantaged upon release. This financial disadvantage may even lead to a revolving door of reoffending in the form of shoplifting to replace such possessions.

A homeless woman may return to prostitution to regain a roof over her head and thus the vicious cycle of recidivism is perpetuated. Certainly there is not much evidence that "prison works" to quote Michael Howard, for women. Women who are already drawn from the financially disadvantaged sector of society cannot possibly be helped to become upwardly mobile by a spell in prison. Furthermore Every Child Matters according to a government Green Paper so why should the children also be indirectly punished ?

Statistics show that severe child poverty is often a consequence of parental imprisonment. Children suffer in other ways too, such as enduring playground taunts and bullying if their peers discover the truth behind a Mother` s absence from school events such as sports day and school plays. Home Office research has shown that 66% of women in prison have dependent children aged under eighteen.

There are currently about forty infants in Mother and Baby Units in England. That is forty little lives that will potentially become ruined by the patriarchal sentencing culture that sanctioned such cruelty
Clearly one can understand why Baroness Corston wishes to see that all women`s prisons are closed. Holloway Prison had damning reports of mice and pigeon droppings in an unannounced visit by Her Majesty`s Chief Inspectorate of Prisons.

A Report commissioned by the Home Office after the suicide of six women in Styal prison, the Corston Report, (Morris 2007) found similar degradation. Such unsavoury living conditions with open lavatories next to food areas, self harm and frequent suicides provide a compelling argument for the closure of prisons housing all women. Many women are sent to prison for non payment of fines some incurred for transgressions such as not having a T. V. licence making poverty a crime in a disturbing echo of the Dickensian days of Debtors Prison.

The population of women in prison is over-represented by duped drug-mule foreign BME groups(CLINKS), and their non violent offences differ from that of male offending. Women tend to commit fewer crimes than men in every area except for prostitution, the latter offense often driven by financial necessity. Such need-driven offending is in stark contrast to the thrill seeking, testosterone fuelled, "doing gender" that often characterises male offending.

The fact that more women are being sent to prison than ever before is also indicative of the prevailing punitive sentencing culture towards women. Reforming, humanitarian organisations such as the Corston Independent Funders Coalition and the Howard League for Penal Reform would both like to see far fewer women sent to prison for such reasons.

The exception to this rule of course would apply to deranged, dangerous women such as Myra Hindley ,Rose West and the nurse Beverly Allitt who murdered several babies in her care. In such exceptional cases of violent female offending then clearly prison is the best solution for the protection of society. However one could also argue that such offenders are in fact mentally ill and should be in a mental institution for dangerous offenders.

Rough Justice:

Let us now briefly look at two high profile cases of rough justice meted out to women in Courts of Law in support of our argument. Firstly let us examine the high profile case of solicitor Sally Clark who was sent to prison for allegedly killing her two baby sons. Her two children tragically died from SIDS (Sudden Infant Death Syndrome) otherwise known as cot death.

An Expert Witness was called to give evidence at her trial. She was subsequently convicted of murder in 1999 and sentenced to prison

thereby compounding her suffering. Expert Witness, Professor Roy Meadows asserted that the odds of two cot deaths occurring were in the region of 73 million to one. Faced with such an impressive figure the jury had no hesitation in finding her guilty.
The Royal society of Statistics realised that Meadow`s use of statistics was completely erroneous and the probabilities cited were fallacious.

Meadow`s cavalier, and reckless use of statistics cost him his reputation. Sally Clark was released but never recovered from her ordeal and tragically died a few years later from alcoholism, leaving her husband bereft. Even if Sally Clark *was in fact guilty* she may have been suffering from a serious medical condition known as post partum psychosis and therefore should not have been sentenced to prison. Here we have a compelling argument for the closure of prisons for women since many may have arrived there due to "rough justice" and an androcentric stereotyping of flawed mothers and "doubly deviant" women. This "judicial logic that sentences them as flawed women rather than lawbreaking citizens" provides another compelling case for the closure of prisons for women.

Another high profile recent case to support our argument, involves a woman in Wales who was sentenced to eight months in prison this year for allegedly perverting the course of justice. This mother of four young children made a complaint of rape against her husband and appears to have been a victim of domestic violence.

She retracted her statement after coercion from her husband who persuaded her that he would receive a seven year sentence if he were to be convicted while she would likely be let off with a caution. This element of male coercion has often resulted in women becoming unwilling partners in crime so to speak and has been analysed by criminologists. In this case Dyfed –Powys Police decided to go ahead with the prosecution resulting in Judge John Rogers, Q.C. passing a prison sentence on this unfortunate rape victim. Here we have a classic example of the punitive and patriarchal excesses of the criminal justice system towards women.

The husband then gained full custody of the children and now this victim, having been released on appeal, is fighting to regain her children. There are no prisons in Wales for women and therefore visits will be extremely difficult where young children are involved. Children will be distressed after a long journey when they see their Mother behind bars and suffer nightmares consequent to such visits. This case has put the sanctity of court proceedings above the welfare of the children and their Mother.

The End Violence Against Women Coalition, said the case sent out a chilling message to rape victims. The woman in question stated that her husband had completely controlled her in every way. This domestic rape victim`s family life and future employment prospects may now be ruined by a prison record (NACRO Change the Record Campaign) while her husband appears to have got off scot free.

Amanda Knox Case:

Another high profile female case that falls outside U.K. Jurisdiction is that of Amanda Knox sentenced to twenty six years in an Italian prison, despite a complete lack of forensic evidence in the crime scene to implicate her. She received the longest sentence of the three suspects; the male offender, drug dealer Rudy Guede was sentenced to sixteen years despite forensic evidence of his semen found in murder victim Meredith. Knox has been sexualised by a media keen to sell newspapers in a “babes behind bars” fashion and received such huge media coverage that her trial was inevitably prejudiced.

The Prosecutor, Giuliano Mignini, is facing charges of corruption (Sunday Times report by Richard Owen). He allegedly consulted a fortune teller prior to the notorious ”Foxy Knoxy” trial. The crystal ball told him that the murder was a sex game gone wrong. Such flimsy supernatural evidence should not have influenced due process in a

Court of Law. It is reminiscent of the sixteenth century days of the Witch Finder General , the Malleus Maleficarum .
One has to question also the calibre of prison activities provided for Knox as she was encouraged to write a short story about a party rape for a prison story competition. Complaints about prison activities generally, extend to gendered domestic cookery classes that stereotype women.
These cases provide *pressing support for closure* of women`s prisons. A wealth of feminist criminology theory describes this judicial victimisation of women and gendered justice.
This sentencing severity towards women may be examined in an historical context when women were disenfranchised and considered demure second class, subservient citizens. In the last century there were no women in Parliament and *men only* made the Laws. Women such as Labour politician Harriett Harman and the Fawcett Society have striven to redress the inequality. The Equality Act of this year (Government Equalities Office) is the latest endeavour of Harriet Harman to ensure fairness. Yet it seems that latent discrimination towards women and their social standing still runs deep within our Courts.

This gendered criminal justice argument provides compelling support for women`s prison closure since many women do not appear to receive a fair or even chivalrous trial . Frances Crook, Director of the Howard League of Penal Reform would like to see a swift programme of women`s prison closure and Lord Leveson, of the Sentencing Council has been ordered to promote this leniency in a time of drastic budget cuts .

Finally, the infamous Stanford Prison experiment shows how those in a position of authority, be they magistrates, judges or students masquerading as "prison guards" are easily tempted to abuse their power .A similar humiliation occurs in women`s prisons with strip searches and mandatory urine tests for drugs that are intrusive and highly embarrassing. Prison guards are not trained as counsellors either and so may be unable to offer emotional support.

To conclude, there is *no evidence* that prison "works" for women and each prison place costs forty five thousand pounds. A growing consensus suggests that instead of prison most women should be allowed to attend friendly community centres. To further this aim the Justice Minister Ken Clark, would like to see a" rehabilitation revolution" in a pragmatic, target-driven, private sector investment approach utilising dividends to reduce recidivism. More investment is essential in community projects that empower women for successful prison closure.

Chapter Four: Impact of Prison on Families

This chapter will explore the pernicious effects on family members when loved ones fall victim to the excesses of criminal justice systems and are sent to prison.
Today one often hears the term Every Child Matters. The Government has a stated provision to ensure that each and every child has the basic requisites to enjoy a happy and enriched childhood. Indeed it has published a Green Paper in 2003 outlining all the provisions for a childhood free from poverty and discrimination and insecurity.

Having sat on a school Governing Board I became very familiar with the expression that Every Child Matters. It was an ideal to which we all aspired to facilitate. When a biometric system was introduced by us against the students` wishes it was sabotaged by a disgruntled attendee who objected to the Orwellian implications of finger printing children! A piece of gum was stuck n the finger printing gadget and that was then end of the biometric attendance system!

It seems apparent that the rights of children to a joyous childhood are *not* being considered within our Criminal Justice system either as record numbers of parents and children are currently incarcerated according to Home Office Statistics. The prison charity CLINKS has a campaign to Make Every Child Matter (MECM) to assist prisoner families.

Maternal Deprivation:

What effects will enforced prison separation have on children deprived of their parent or parent deprived of their child? There are numerous deleterious consequences to be considered. Adverse psychological effects indisputably arise when a child experiences separation from a primary caregiver. These have been researched by Professor John Bowlby who studied the effect of separation of infants from their Mothers.

The idea of maternal deprivation has gained much credence in psychological circles and has been posited as being a contributory factor to delinquency. Jailed Mothers in America cite separation from their children as the worst part of the sentence. Baroness Corston feels that all women`s prisons should be closed for such reasons.. Frances Crook the Director of the Howard League for Penal Reform is petitioning for removal of young women within the criminal justice system after six suicides in HMP Styal including a young girl who left her mother heartbroken.

The expression "affectionless sociopath" derived from Bowlby`s seminal work. The theory surmises that disruption of the emotional bonding process can lead to irrevocable consequences for the child and his or her behaviour later in life. The child who has endured the trauma of such separation may have difficulty in forming emotional attachments later to others and exhibit a lack of empathy that is said to be the hallmark of sociopathic or psychopathic behaviour.

If there are frequent changes and abandonment by successive carers then the outcome may be a damaged child who will forever feel insecure and unloved and in turn be unable to show any real affection to others according to this theory .There have been numerous deaths in custody, and deportation of foreign nationals to distant shores so sometimes this separation can become permanent (INQUEST Statistics).

Therefore according to this stream of academic thought the act of separating a child from a parent may indirectly lead to a greater propensity for that child to become an offender in the future. Thus one can hypothesise that a vicious and detrimental cycle of offending behaviour is perpetuated through the generations as a result of imprisonment. In a quasi biblical sense the sins of the Father are thus visited unto the sons.

Surely a legacy of damaged children is not the outcome that Michael Howard had in mind when he uttered the apocryphal aphorism Prison Works? The Conservative Government of John Major aspired to imbue confidence into the electorate with tough rhetoric and policies on Law and Order at a time of rising crime levels. This penal populism was designed to curry favour with the insecure electorate. One has to be cynical of politicians who manipulate the media in this nefarious way to clamour for a hard line response to those who cross the fine line into crime. How can this tough authoritarian approach possibly assist struggling families?

The term" Prison Works" has seminally given birth to a whole new generation of "What Works" offender studies in a seeming parody of the original expression. Michael Howard certainly made a lasting impact on the criminal justice system with this exhortation! Subsequently record numbers were sentenced to prison. Today the prisons are full to capacity with nearly 84 thousand inmates (HM Prison statistics).
There can be little doubt however that prison *does not work* for the families of those incarcerated.

One of the deleterious consequences of penal retributivism is financial hardship for those family members left on the outside. If the main breadwinner is locked up then a family will lose a substantial source of income. The remaining parent may be unable to work if they are undertaking the role of full time carer to young children. This could result in homelessness or severe child poverty says the Joseph Rowntree Foundation. Homelessness is a condition that successive governments have each promised to eradicate. Prison leads to severe poverty for families.

Visits to distant prisons can be very difficult and costly for prisoner families and FFOPS give advice about travel to prisons and emotional support. Children may find such visits frightening rather than comforting; Prison is not a child friendly environment. Sometimes a parent arrives at Court believing they will *not*receive a custodial sentence and have made no practical preparations such as childcare beforehand. FFOPS can help in such situations by liaising with family and friends to assist the prisoner`s family and help them cope with the sudden shock and chaos in their lives.

There may be problems with paying rent and housing that affect the family members left on the outside. In some cases both parents are sent to prison leaving teenagers to cope on their own.
Another support group is Action for Prisoners Families. They have shown that a family may lose their home and thousands of pounds a year in income as a result of imprisonment. This Government organisation offers an excellent series of publications with titles such as "My Dad is in prison" that are suitable for young children.

Confused and frightened youngsters may exhibit behavioural problems such as nightmares and bed wetting. AFP has a stated vision to ensure that families are protected from discrimination and become involved in the prisoners progress. The sentencing Magistrate or Judge would be wise to heed the counsel that Every Child Matters when passing sentence in a Court of Law. They would be just and equitable to realise that their sentence may cause unnecessary suffering to children, some of whom may even have to be placed in care homes (Home Office Statistics). In poorer countries their families may even starve.

There are some prisons such as HMP Bullingdon in Oxfordshire that offer anger management courses for prisoners. Each prisoner can receive a small payment of five pounds for attending. This will assist their impoverished families who often actually send money to prisoners. Disappointingly it was reported that prison guards were complaining about this small payment as if it were the height of extravagance.

Such incentives should work well according to Skinnerian conditioning theories, and cognitive behavioural approaches to offending .Anger control lessons will also assist their families. The current financial crisis has prompted the present Minister of Justice Kenneth Clarke to propose that inmates work full time and earn the minimum wage which is in the region of twelve thousand pounds a year.

The earnings would go towards the prisoners` upkeep as well as towards their families. It remains to be seen whether this latter promise would be kept as politicians have a history of reneging on their word. If families of prisoners were to receive some of these wages then it would be a most beneficial and provident policy. Somehow one intuitively senses that the prisoners earnings will all end up in the coffers of the cash strapped Ministry of Justice.

It seems indisputable that prison should only be used as a last resort, if at all, when there are dependant family members involved. The only possible justification for such a sentence would be in cases where the offender poses a serious danger to the safety of others. In cases of domestic violence the removal of the offender from the family would clearly be a relief. Sometimes extremely dangerous offenders are best kept removed from their families in order to prevent a tragic crime.

A case that springs to mind is that of Raoul Moat who became infamous for his killing spree as soon as he was released from prison this year. Clearly his incarceration did *not* have a beneficial effect upon his family and his spell inside certainly did *not* result in the steroid user becoming a well behaved and reformed member of society. Indeed it seems woefully apparent that the prison term resulted in extreme resentment and a brooding anger that sparked the catastrophic events that followed. When estranged from his family in prison Moat received the devastating news that his partner was seeing someone else; a supposed policeman!

This is a situation that doubtless occurs frequently in prison life. He embarked on a shooting killing spree and was shot himself with an experimental taser known as the Xrep.

Drugs are rife in Prison:

One may speculate that had Moat not been sent to prison in the first place and taking anabolic steroids inside prison which are proven to cause a syndrome known as `Roid Rage the tragedy would never have occurred. It is widely reported that prison is rife with drug taking and there appears to be little difficulty for prisoners who wish to take drugs of any category.

Clearly this culture of drug taking in prisons is not going to have a beneficial effect on a prisoner`s family. Sometimes a prisoner encounters illicit drugs for the very first time while serving a prison sentence (Green Paper Tackling Drugs Together).The justification for the Prison Works policy does not seem to hold up to critical scrutiny. A prisoner may emerge as a ghostly spectre of his former self after incarceration due to peer influenced drug taking and an unhealthy environment. This deterioration of body and mind will impact negatively on the family.

Some studies have shown a link between a lack of Vitamin D and illnesses such as heart disease and even cancer. Although I am not aware of any research yet into the levels of prisoners Vitamin D one can safely surmise that they will be lower than those on the outside since the vitamin is mainly formed via sunlight falling on the skin If a prisoner becomes ill or even dies as a result of incarceration then clearly this will impact seriously upon the family.

Currently a three year study is taking place in HMP Hindley, under the supervision of Professor John Stein with support from Natural Justice a charity that looks into the causes of offending. If the hypothesis were to be proven that various nutritional supplements improve behaviour then this will surely benefit the prisoner and his family. One awaits the result of this double blind study with interest but somehow one cannot see how such a simplistic approach to offending could hold much water.

Furthermore how many of the prisoners are really bad people whose behaviour needs to be improved by diet? Many have arrived in prison through misfortunes in the punitive criminal justice system, or through **uptariffing and net widening.**

Some are unjustly incarcerated for their political ideologies, as in China, or on the basis of their ethnicity due to discrimination from (SUS) Stop and Search Laws causing their families untold pain. Amnesty International fights for the rights of these prisoners of conscience.

Prison overcrowding can lead to an increased likelihood of aggression and violence. Numerous psychological studies have demonstrated that crowding results in increased hostility and territoriality. One only has to recall how uncomfortable it is to be jostled and pushed in a bustling street to realise that the current prison situation must be intolerable. Many barbaric attacks occur in prison and this is hardly the environment to facilitate rehabilitation. Human beings are fundamentally territorial and need to define their own space .This clearly is difficult in prisons and thus there is an increased risk of violence erupting inside.

The lasting psychological trauma of such vicious attacks, even rapes, *impact harshly on family* members (Johnson 1995).A family may become dysfunctional as a result. A school of thought believes that those who witness aggression may learn to copy such unacceptable behaviour via imitation or social learning.Thus a child may model himself on an incarcerated parent and become an offender in the future .

The Government wants to redress the problem of rising prison numbers by invoking a new culture of leniency in the criminal justice system. The last decades have seen a rapidly rising prison population due to Government policies such as mandatory minimum sentences and longer sentences (HM Prison Statistics).

The problem has been exacerbated by the prevailing sentencing culture of some Magistrates who have been swayed by whim and prejudice rather than the sword of justice. There has been a culture of meting out Indeterminate Sentences for Public Protection known as IPPs, and prisons are bursting at the seams, and at what cost to their families?

The Sentencing Council has been ordered to change its sentencing guidelines to promote this pragmatic leniency.

Lord Justice Leveson, Chairman of the Sentencing Council wishes to see 7000 fewer prison sentences passed by next year as part of the "rehabilitation revolution" drive by Kenneth Clarke. Admittedly the aim of this benign policy may be to save the prison service millions of pounds in a time of drastic budgetary cuts .None the less the outcome of such cost cutting measures may be that *fewer families suffer* indirectly as a result of prison sentences.

It was reported that Prison Governors are none too happy at this proposal to cut prison numbers.

They fear that a proposed reduction of seven thousand inmates would result in prison closures and potential job losses. One hopes that *many families* of prisoners will benefit from the proposed changes, yet if the Prison Governors Association (PGA) has its way this may not happen. The executive of Victim Support, Owen Sharp was also quoted as saying "victims want sentences they feel are fair". The ideals of reforming organisations such as the Howard League for Penal Reform, and the Corston Independent Funders Coalition, have many hurdles to surmount not least the PGA and Victim Support.

From a historical perspective the quest to protect families from the adverse effects of imprisonment can be traced to prison reformers such as John Howard and Quaker Elisabeth Fry. The shocking conditions of prisons in the eighteenth century led to the far reaching reforms instigated by John Howard and to the present Howard League of Penal Reform. Today the organisation is vibrant with enthusiasm from its student campaigning members.

The Howard League had a pre-election campaign called Take Action 2010 which called for "less crime, safer communities, fewer people in prison". England and Wales lock up more children than any other country in Europe causing untold anguish to their families. If John Howard were alive today one can imagine how proud he would be at continued reform attempts bearing his name. Yet there are still children as young as ten behind bars in our current penal system causing suffering to grandparents, siblings, and non- nuclear extended family networks.

Children in custody are serving longer sentences according to the sentencing statistics for England and Wales . The Chair of the Youth Justice Board said that" twice as many children were locked up as a decade ago despite the fact that the British crime Survey recorded a 44 per cent decline in crime,
The pernicious effect on the family of child imprisonment is not hard to imagine. The use of victim offender reparative mediation or restorative justice and targeted probation projects based on cognitive behaviour therapy is surely preferable to incarceration for the prisoner families.
A ten year old child should be tucked up snugly in bed with her dolls and is surely doli incapax?

The Law Lords have a lot to answer for when they decided to reduce the age of criminal responsibility to ten years of age in our country (Crime and Disorder Act 1998). In 1850 a ten year old boy was sent to prison for playing with his spinning top in a public place and annoying someone. This poignant anecdote immediately brings to mind the uncomfortable comparison with our present day penal system, where children are incarcerated, some of whom may be asylum seekers. This is manifestly unjust and very bad for their schooling and education. Asylum detention centres such as Campsfield are in effect prisons.

Even as far back in time as 1850 it was soon agreed that the age of children to be summarily tried should be raised to sixteen (Prison Timelines).We seem to have regressed here. The age of criminal responsibility should be raised to at least sixteen as psychological studies have indicated that teenage brains are still maturing.

Since young minds are not fully mature they should not be detained in custody according to neuro-cognitive research. Using MRI scanners researchers have demonstrated that there are measurable changes taking place in the frontal and parietal lobes of the teenage brain that have profound implications for criminal justice. These brain structures are responsible for executive self control. If these structures are still maturing it could partly explain teenage impulsive behaviour. This rewiring is not perfected until the late teens to early twenties.

These empirical research findings could be used as a legitimate defence in a Court of Law for unruly teen behaviour. It is therefore profoundly wrong according to this research to give ASBO`S or incarcerate young offenders, causing *untold damage* to their families and future careers. In the nineteenth century there were many cases of whole families being locked up together in Debtors Prisons. These institutions for the poor were vividly described by the author Charles Dickens in works such as “Little Dorrit” in the Marshalsea.

One might hope that in this supposedly enlightened century of ours that debt would no longer be a crime deserving of incarceration. Surely the concept of debt meriting a custodial sentence must belong to the past?

Sadly this is not strictly the case in the political economy of Late Modernity and a society sadly still redolent with Capitalist values.

The title of Jeffrey Reiman`s 1984 critique "the rich get richer and the poor get prison" so eloquently sums up this attitude to the disadvantaged in our materialistic and hierarchical society.
Mothers have even been sent to Holloway prison for fines incurred as a result of not having a television licence. An article in the Independent newspaper (Cohen 1994) revealed that 894 people had been jailed in the previous year for this offense resulting in criticism of the Home office and T.V, licensing authority.

The very high fine imposed for this transgression is often beyond the means of poorer women. Being faced with the option of paying one thousand pounds or a short spell inside, many impoverished mothers are forced into the latter option causing devastation to their families. Here is an example of how the criminal justice system is biased against the less affluent members of society. In other words the Dickensian days of Debtors prison are still with us today and causing *untold suffering to countless families*.

It is also shocking that women have been sent to prison whilst pregnant and have been forced to give birth while shackled to the delivery bed. There are eight mother and baby units in prisons. Infants are cruelly wrenched from their mothers when they reach eighteen months. Childbirth is a time of the utmost vulnerability that may not be understood by a punitive masculine system. The patriarchal culture that has sanctioned this cruelty towards women and infants desperately needs attention and reform.

One cannot underestimate the emotional pain of such abrupt infant separations. The long term repercussions and stigma of a prison sentence on the family is also enormous. There are around 150,000 children in England and Wales affected by this painful issue or 7% of all schoolchildren say the Prison Reform Trust. Those who feel marginalised from society sense rejection by their peers. A child may have to endure taunts and mockery in the school playground when his peers discover that his parent is behind bars. In effect the child is suffering his own comparable sentence .These traumatic memories may persist throughout their lives.

There is also a danger of a state of passive resignation known as learned helplessness occurring. This behavioural phenomenon was discovered by Martin Seligman in his experiments with unrelenting stress. Much the same behaviour has been found in people who feel that they are not in control of their environment. Studies have shown they become demoralised to a point whereby they feel that nothing they do will ameliorate the predicament they are trapped in. They become apathetically resigned to their fate and simply give up trying to effect an improvement in their surroundings. This is why families of prisoners need to be given the utmost support to avoid sinking into apathy and social exclusion. These pernicious effects may be life long, a true life sentence in every sense of the words.

This lifelong effect on the family can extend to the domain of future employment. Once a prisoner is released it will be much harder for he or she to re-enter the job market. Despite the euphemistic aims of the Rehabilitation of Offenders Act, 1974, many ex convicts are discriminated against in the jobs market. Employers routinely call for criminal records checks even when there is no real need for them. This is an issue that charitable organisations such as NACRO are presently trying to address, with the launch of their Change the Record Campaign.

Much needs to be done in this area if the needs of prisoners` families are to be met. Reintegration into society is crucial to the future well being of the family unit. Social Inclusion Units aim to encourage strong family relationships to help prevent prisoners reoffending .Inclusion Units believe that poverty results in prisoner family exclusion from group activities and therefore offer support. Such support groups are crucial to the well being of prisoner families. A well paid job will enhance the prospects of the family staying together as divorce is often a consequence of incarceration both during the sentence and after release according to Action for Prisoners Family support group.

APF feel that an empirically based research strategy needs to be implemented as a foundation for the edifice of prisoner family support (B. The support group (APF) is looking for research that will achieve best policy and best practice with the aim to reduce recidivism. Two thirds reoffend after release indicating the prison regime *does not work*. This is why a payment-by-results or a rehabilitation revolution is the latest trend with the Ministry of Justice . However the problems families face within the criminal justice system are not just confined to our shores.

USA Extradition Treaty:

In 2003 a controversial Extradition Treaty became law enabling the removal of British citizens to face justice elsewhere. This clearly would cause a *great deal of suffering to families* and there has been a high profile case involving a devoted campaigning mother and her son, Gary McKinnon. Gary suffers from Asperger`s Disorder.

His main crime was to demonstrate the flaws in the U. S. military computer system by successfully hacking into it while searching for evidence of alien life! This intelligent, autistic man might have been condemned to sixty years in a harsh American jail if he had been extradited. Many legal experts feel that this Treaty is inherently prejudicial and one sided and should be reviewed. Well at least this is how the British see it!!! Needless to say this approach might not go down to well with the American government that rightly wishes to protect its valuable military computers from cyber crime!

Detention without Charge:

Campaign groups such as Liberty are concerned about the Human rights implications of this treaty. Shami Chakrabarti is the Director of Liberty. She also campaigned against Habeas Corpus and detention without charge for 42 days in with David Davis in the Haltemprice by election. Campaign group Liberty have argued that if innocent people were locked up for six weeks as suspected terrorists they could lose their homes if the mortgage was not paid causing a family schism. Most detainees are subsequently exonerated. The stigma by association that families of serious offenders endure has been thoroughly described in an excellent study by Rachel Condry with the now disbanded Aftermath Project.
There is usually an assumption that a prisoner is guilty despite the fact that miscarriages of justice occur. Such “rough justice” causes *untold distress to families*. A recent world wide political and media furore erupted following the plea for clemency from the children of an Iranian prisoner, Sakineh Ashtiani.

Her children wrote to the press in a frantic bid to save their Mother from being stoned to death after a trumped up charge of adultery. There seems to be little evidential basis against this widow and the actual convicted killer of her husband has been released. It seems that she has become a scapegoat for the crime purely because she is a woman. Her teenage children are suffering because of the misogynistic zeitgeist in the Iranian criminal justice system.

The Sharia Law system believes in an “eye for an eye” and blood thirsty revenge; especially against women (Women against Sharia 2010). This comparative example gives us a small snapshot of the immeasurable suffering experienced by countless families all over the world when their loved ones are imprisoned without due process, and concludes this analysis of the suffering of prisoner families. In an ideal world such familial suffering would be considered by those passing sentence.

Chapter Five: Islamic State Radicalisation of Prisoners

This chapter will discuss a new threat that is evolving inside prisons today, namely that of home grown terrorism caused by conversion to *radical* Islam as opposed to the usual and prevalent, peaceful doctrine of Islam. It will propose aetiological reasons for this worrying phenomenon that is proliferating in prisons and examine what counter measures, if any, are being implemented.

In 2018 the statistics show that there are at least 700 Islamist extremists in British jails alone. Doubtless the same scenario might be occurring in other nations` prisons. In some prisons the entire Muslim population has been segregated to form a separate prison wing in order to curtail the spread of radicalised ideas. There has been an increase in prisoners who have been convicted of terrorist offences and this is also fuelling a problem of radicalisation taking place amongst inmates.

This rise in the Muslim prison population has meant that prison officers are now being trained in spotting the signs of radicalised and dangerous beliefs. There are now at least 13, 000 Muslim prisoners incarcerated in England alone. This is a very large percentage and is causing concern amongst the prison governors.

One of Britain`s most notorious prisoners is Anjem Choudary who became infamous for his Finsbury mosque speeches and rants against westerners. His speeches crossed the line of law and order and he was accused of terrorism offences and of inciting unrest and of trying to radicalise Muslim people against the western culture of democracy in which they live. Anjem Choudhary has now been placed in one of the new religious separation units in Frankland Prison. The fiery preacher had called for Muslims to support the creation of a caliphate which is the same aim of the Islamic State fighters in Syria and other middle eastern countries.

The fighters for Islamic State have tried albeit unsuccessfully to create a world that is ruled by a caliphate. This caliphate is a state that is governed by the repressive rule of Sharia law. The ultimate goal and aim of ISIS who are also known as Daesh, is for Sharia Law to replace other legal systems and to become the dominant legal system in the entire world. Sharia law is one of the most repressive and regressive legal systems in the world.

Sharia strips women of their fundamental right to be treated as equals to their male counterparts. Under repressive Sharia laws women are mere second class citizens that have to subserviently obey their husbands. Sharia has very strict so called modesty rules that mean a woman has to be covered up from head to toe. The all- covering garment known as the Burkha is an example of how the modesty laws prevent a woman from exposing any part of her body in public.

Sharia laws are also very brutal. Any person found guilty of adultery can be stoned to death under Sharia laws. Even minor transgressions can result in the death penalty.

There are cases of disgruntled relatives telling tales about their family members to the authorities in order to get a disliked relative executed. The Sharia courts of law are not known for leniency nor for listening to the facts and evidence. Another crime that merits a death sentence is witch craft or apostacy. Again many people have been put to death and executed in a barbaric fashion, on mere hear say. Any person who accidentally swears about the Holy God Mohammed can be put to death. Sometimes young teenagers have accidentally made unwise comments on facebook and have been executed. Every single word is monitored closely under Sharia laws.

Sharia is a patriarchal legal system that favours the male. Therefore one can appreciate why Sharia is popular amongst the dominant male ISIS group. Sharia even permits the fighters of Islamic State to have extramarital sex for the good of the cause. There have been women kidnapped as sex slaves in Syria. An American aid worker was kidnapped and used as a sex slave in Syria. Her name was Kayla Mueller and she was captured and held by the iSIS leader Abu Bakr Al Bagdadi. Sharia laws allow the exploitation of women and it is hardly surprising that Sharia is becoming so popular among certain criminal factions including the radicalised prison population.

It is very concerning that here in Great Britain there are many Sharia Courts that are operating alongside our own British legal system. It seems that the British government is so keen to bow to political correctness that they may have over stepped a line of common sense. Many of the terrorists who later committed bombing atrocities have appeared on British television calling for Sharia Law to prevail in the United Kingdom. Indeed one of the London bridge terrorists had appeared on television calling for Sharia law to be introduced here before he committed the atrocity.

As an aside I would like to say that President Trump is on the right track with his concerns about the radical form of Islam. However he is rather naive in the way he puts forward his beliefs and this has caused him to seem a little politically incorrect at times. A politician has to tread a very line even when voicing wholly legitimate concerns. Donald Trump is correct in his concerns over the spread of radical Islam.

In Europe alone there are at least 70, 000 dangerously radicalised Islamists who are prepared to wage an allegedly religious Holy War that is also known as Jihad. A Jihadi religious fighter can legitimately kill anyone who is a Christian, a Jew or even simply not a proper hard line Muslim as it is allowed by the rules of Jihad. Most moderate Muslims abhor the idea of any form of killing in the name of religion and therefore one cannot tar all Muslims with the same brush.

The dangers of its legal system are very apparent. However a politician simply cannot cast aspersions on a whole ethnic community and one must remember that many Muslims are very moderate in their views and do subscribe to the hard line tenets of Sharia law. Here in Great Britain there are many attempts to build cohesion amongst all creeds and faiths and to make the Muslim community feel integrated and a welcome part in society.

However there have been concerns raised about schools known as Madrassas. These schools are found all over the word and are proliferating here in Great Britain. There have been concerns about the teaching of radical beliefs and the indoctrination of young children in these Madrassas. Some Madrassas in the Middle East have been used as training grounds for future fighters for the Islamic state factions. Some of these highly trained fighters have managed to return to Great Britain and have ended up in the prison system. Before the present system of separation was introduced there were many cases of radicalised prisoners being able to exert their influence over other prisoners.

Prison is an environment that exacerbates feelings of extreme vulnerability and a loss of identity. A prisoner is stripped of many of his accoutrements that are part of his daily life on the outside. Many choices are removed from a prisoner such as food and clothing. There have been numerous psychological studies that demonstrate the adverse effects of feeling disempowered. Therefore those who are affiliated with the powerful Islamic state fighters will feel extremely empowered and bold. Many western prisoners convert in prison to become Muslim in order to feel part of a perceived powerful group.

These studies showed how a phenomenon known as “learned helplessness” may occur in an oppressive environment from which no escape is possible. This condition can lead to extreme apathy and a realisation that the situation is a hopeless one. The malaise experienced in these situations is very unpleasant and painful.

Therefore any course of action that serves to counteract these feelings of impotence will seem very attractive. Prisoners feel completely disempowered and therefore they are ripe for conversion to the cause of Jihad. The waging of a righteous battle against the unworthy Infidel might appeal to those who feel completely disempowered. This would especially make sense when one considers that this infidel is responsible for the plight of incarceration which is causing the prisoner to suffer.

A famous experiment demonstrated how those in a position of power are easily tempted to abuse their power. This was the Stanford prison experiment where students masqueraded as prison guards while fellow students assumed the role of prisoners. The student prison guards became so inebriated with their omnipotence that they started to abuse the pretend prisoners and the experiment had to be halted.

Therefore one may deduce that real life prisoners run a risk of being bullied by the omnipotent prison guards. From a psychological point of view it makes perfect sense that these feelings of disengagement might propel the actor along the path of terrorism with a little persuasion. Prison is a painful environment. This suffering may engender a desire for retribution against the perpetrator. Prison therefore provides a perfect breeding ground for *Islamist radicalisation.*

The waging of a Holy War, known as Jihad, may serve to empower those who were previously feeling powerless. Prison conditions of under staffing as well as over- crowding, might facilitate this process. Many prisoners fear victimisation and may even be raped or assaulted. There is some truth in the saying that there is safety in numbers.

Those who join the religious groups in prison will immediately feel protected by the peer group. The prisoner will no longer feel isolated and fearful. Initially there will be a sensation of relief that there is membership of a united cohesive group that is providing religious teachings. The process of *radicalisation* may possibly follow later; sometimes it will emerge years later. It is important to stress that there is a dearth of empirical research in this area.

The ability to be influenced by one`s peers was examined by the criminologist Edwin Sutherland. He called his theory "differential association". Many small self starting independent Jihad groups are forming in prison via social bonding processes. Individuals behave differently in groups as they feel empowered by the group .

The idea that groups behave more recklessly as an entity has been labelled the "risky shift" by social psychologists. The phenomenon is also known as group polarisation. Prisoners often hail from a gang culture, especially those in Supermax prisons in the U.S. Many gang members have tattoos expressing their gang allegiance. Gang culture readily lends itself to the conversion to *radical* Islam.

Islam is now the fastest growing religion in prisons and 240.0000 inmates have converted to Islam in American prisons since the 9/11 attacks (Hamm 2009). However it is important to note that there is absolutely nothing wrong with conversion to Islam. The problem purely lies with the phenomenon of *radicalisation.*

Just as prisons are often considered to be schools for crime so they may be considered to be schools for *radical* Islam. Many prisoners had no prior inclination towards religiosity prior to their conversion in prison. Islam professes to be a peaceful religion and is not in itself the cause of radicalisation. However certain tenets of the Koran are very worrying. The tenets include the ideal of stamping out Christianity and Judaism worldwide, as well as eliminating homosexuality.

There are worrisome issues regarding equality and diversity in these days of equality laws. Muslim women are treated as having fewer rights in contravention of accepted diversity laws. Sharia Law has made substantial inroads into British jurisprudence and there are Sharia courts operating here. Sharia courts deal with divorce matters in a completely different way. A husband may easily rid himself of a tiresome wife in a perfunctory hearing but the converse does not apply. Clearly there are serious implications of this gradual encroachment on our legal system.

A group of prisoners that had converted to Islam were interviewed in British prisons by Howard League researchers. Those who took part said they felt it had given them moral strength and a sense of purpose. One has to remember that Islam forbids drinking alcohol as well as drug taking and therefore it can impose a self discipline that hitherto had been lacking (Spalek & El-Hassain 2007). However one must consider that many *radical* Islamists would refuse to even communicate with non believers, who they designate as "kuffar" or infidels.

The Koran also says "do not take the Jews and Christians for your friends (Q, 5:51). Therefore this sample that cooperated with the interviewers would have been biased towards the less extremist end of the spectrum.

The powerful sense of superiority conveyed by elitist teachings might appeal to a prisoner experiencing low self esteem and disempowerment. The prison service and the CJS have been shown to be institutionally racist after the Lawrence enquiry and many prisoners will be justified in nursing a grievance. The prison service also facilitated the racist murder of Zahid Mubarak in his cell.

Therefore the creed of Jihad has a few elements that may appeal to angry male prisoners and give justification for acts of violence against non Muslims. However it must be stressed that most of the teachings are very enlightened, worthy and spiritual and very few converts embark on this path.

The thwarted airline bomber, Richard Reid, was *radicalised i*nside Feltham young Offenders institution. In 2001 London born Richard Reid tried to blow up a transatlantic jet airliner with a bomb hidden inside his shoe. He became known as the "shoe bomber" and subsequently all American airline passengers must now remove their shoes for inspection before boarding a flight. Richard Reid the shoe bomber joined al-Qaeda with encouragement from the Brixton and Finsbury Mosques and embarked on the failed suicide mission.

His plot failed and he is currently incarcerated inside a Supermax prison. Reid converted to Islam while in Feltham and after his release he listened to the preaching of anti-American cleric Abu Hamza in Finsbury Mosque. In 1999 Abu Hamza gave a sermon in Arabic exhorting the murder of the infidel wherever they may be. He was also arrested that year for involvement with the murder of tourists in Yemen and preached to fellow inmates before being released.

The bomber of July 7 2005, Mohammed Sidique Khan, also attended *radical* sermons preached by Abu Hamza at Finsbury mosque in 2004. The London bombers also went on a team building outdoor pursuits expedition to the Lake district and the Brecon Beacons. The idea of such group activities is to form strong allegiance and group identity. Team building and outdoor exercise is routinely used by companies to improve staff morale and interpersonal cooperation.
Two weeks after the tragic London bombings there was another attempt to blow up London transport by six different jihadists, once again planned to take place on Thursday.

Thursday is often the favoured day for suicide bombers as they believe that it will enable their souls to enter paradise on the Friday, their holy day. There they will be greeted by a bevy of female virgins. The Islamic paradise is described in great sensual detail in the Koran. It is a place overflowing with fine wine, jewels and seductive dark eyed virgins. The Koran also praises and encourages martyrdom. It is easy to imagine that a sex starved prisoner might be won over by such promises in the after life!

There was speculation that the leader, Muktar Said Ibrahim, of the July 21 2005 fertiliser bomb plot had previously been *radicalised* while serving time in prison for an offence of assault on a young girl. Muktar

Said Ibrahim is now serving a forty year sentence and is considered a risk to the other prisoners by security services because of his belligerent views. There is concern that he will radicalise a substantial number of his fellow inmates.

Other dangerous jihadists behind bars include the leader of the 2006 plot to blow up seven airliners with explosives disguised as liquid drinks. The Home Office think tank, named Quilliam is concerned that al-Qaeda is recruiting jihadists from behind bars. Quilliam assert that Abu Qatada has issued Fatwas, religious commands, from his cell in Long Larten Prison. He used the internet to do this. Abu Qatada, is considered by MI5 to be a delegate of Osama bin Laden. He has called for the murder of infidels and of moderate Muslims. Quilliam believes that an increasingly volatile situation is being completely mismanaged and misread by the Prison Service.

Meanwhile the bellicose cleric, Abu Hamza has been using the central heating pipes that connect the cells to deliver inflammatory *radical* sermons in Belmarsh prison. He was finally sentenced to prison in 2006 after years of coordinating atrocities such as the murders in Yemen. Also in Belmarsh prison fighting extradition to France for years was the leader of the Paris metro bomb which killed eight people in 1995. Rachid Ramda had even been allowed to lead Friday prayers in Belmarsh before he was extradited indicating that extremists are running rings around a beleaguered prison service.

Al-Qaeda is Arabic for the word “base” and is an umbrella group of twenty extremist factions headed by Osama bin Laden. On conversion bomber Richard Reid changed his appearance and he grew his beard long. The adoption of unique and differing dress codes is analogous to the specific tattoos worn by gang members. It gives a sense of belonging to a powerful club and of being different to others. It is the opposite of integration.

It is practicing a type of elitism. The members feel a sense of privilege in belonging to an exclusive club. People like to conform. Being an insider is always preferable to the stigma of being an outsider. Those who share common values and dress codes develop bonds that are augmented by opposition to those who hold conflicting values. It is practicing a type of segregation from the community which then makes it easier to attack its members.

Recently Professor Michael Clarke warned that up to 800 radicalised prisoners will soon be released in Britain and possibly pose a security risk (Clarke 2010). Professor Clarke of the National Security Forum fears that a new wave of lone wolf attacks may erupt in contrast to the larger coordinated terrorist attacks as seen on the World Trade Center.

The Ministry of Justice queried the figure of 800 radicalised inmates and the assertion that prisons were becoming “universities of terror”. The Ministry stated that of the 6000 inmates in the high security estate there were not as many converts as Professor Michael had supposed. However the Ministry of Justice did not consider the lower prison categories where there are around ten thousand Muslims, when making their deduction.

A small cohort of prisoners with violent tendencies may choose to adopt a bellicose approach to their new found faith. It is very important to reiterate that most religious converts will not embark on a Jihad mission when released. It is the very few that may possibly pose a security risk. Currently the proportion of inmates converting to Islam stands at three times higher than that of the Muslim population on the outside. There are about ten thousand Muslim prisoners in prisons in England and Wales, the majority of whom are peaceful and spiritual.

In category A Whitemoor Prison the percentage is much higher still and more prisoners are converted on a daily basis. There are at least 150 converts in Whitemoor and they are considered to be really “cool” according to a prison officer. It is important to observe that converting to Islam does not automatically imply a path to radicalism or Jihad. Islam preaches many worthy doctrines such as the avoidance of drugs and alcohol. This is in stark contrast to the undisciplined culture of substance abuse in the West that is considered debauched by converts. Hence nightclubs that sell alcohol have been considered to be legitimate targets.

Whitemoor prison is a high security prison in Cambridgeshire where three quarters of inmates have been convicted of murder or are serving indeterminate sentences for public protection. The Friday prayer service at Whitemoor represents the biggest regular gathering of high risk and dangerous prisoners in the entire country. Professor Alison Liebling is Director of Cambridge University Prison Research Centre. She feels concerned about the nascent situation of radicalisation in Whitemoor. Some prisoners convert for self preservation as the religious groups offer protection.

In Whitemoor a non violent Muslim prisoner complained about their violent interpretation of peaceful Islam. He was subsequently stabbed by the incensed purist inmates for taking such a mild view. This incident tends to corroborate the premise that inmates are becoming dangerously radicalised warriors rather than paragons of religious virtue. Clearly not all of the converts will embark on a path of destruction and Jihad, though certain verses of the Koran state unbelievers deserve to have their throats cut. This animosity is especially directed towards Christians and those of the Jewish faith. Maybe this is why Jewish born Alison Liebling spoke of having terrifying nightmares after her visit to HMP Whitemoor.

The anxious Prison Service has now been using psychologists to advise prisoner Imams on how to counteract this trend. The criminologist David Wilson felt that Imams were not stoking the problem in prisons with their benign and harmless teachings in 2001. Professor Wilson has studied the role of Imams within the prison system .On the other hand two Imams were dismissed from prison because of their anti-American comments. One has to appreciate that there is a valid reason for such anti American sentiment in the light of terrible abuses by American soldiers in Abu Ghraib prison in Iraq. The Home Office employs around thirty five Imams for prisoners as Islam is now the second largest religious group in prison today.

Several American hostages were videoed being beheaded in Iraq by al-Zarqawi in 2004. Al-Zarqawi had been previously sent to prison for petty street crime and while inside he read the Koran and emerged calling himself a religious leader.

Islam is essentially an imperialistic doctrine and preaches that lands of the infidel should be conquered. This jingoistic aim has been borne out by the historical records which estimate that around sixty million Christians and Jews have been killed in Holy Wars waged since the middle ages. The Christians are also somewhat guilty of religious extremism with their infamous crusades..

Bellicose angry sentiments against Christians might appeal to prisoners who may have tendencies to antisocial behaviour or be at an arrested infantile stage of moral development . However one must stress that the human rights abuses in Abu Ghraib are a legitimate reason for such anger against the Infidel.

It has been noted that some DSPD (dangerous, severe, personality disorder) offenders have a triad of behaviours that includes a fascination with setting fires and childhood cruelty to animals. This is known as the MacDonald triad and has been used to predict sociopathic behaviour by criminologists.

The desire to cause explosions via terrorist acts could be considered as a manifestation of this fire starting sociopathic behaviour. There is also a worrying link between terrorism and organised crime .

A Fatwa is a “holy command”. It has been shown in various experiments that people will obey commands to commit heinous acts if such requests emanate from a perceived legitimate authority.

A famous experiment demonstrating unquestioning obedience to authority took place in 1963 where volunteers were happy to administer painful electric shocks to hapless subjects, despite their screams for mercy. The shocks were faked and no one was actually electrocuted. The post war study took place in the context of the Holocaust to try and understand why people obey orders to commit evil deeds. The study was disguised as a fake learning experiment, and the learners were in fact stooges.

The sociologist Stanley Milgram was intrigued when the defendants at the Nuremburg trials said that they were "just obeying orders". The conclusion was that many people will unthinkingly obey commands from legitimate authority figures even to do harm, as we are hard wired for obedience. This finding has worrisome implications for this analysis of *radicalisation* and obedience to commands known as Fatwas. It is important to note the distinction between moderate Islam and the term *radicalisation* to avoid any offence to the holy religion of Muslims. Furthermore, one must note that many Muslims have also been victims of terrorist acts, as in 9/11 and the London bombings.
The conclusion of this analysis is that the Prison Service should maintain a critical eye on the situation while simultaneously respecting the religious rights and freedoms of worship of prisoners.

Chapter Six: too Mad for Prison?

This chapter will examine the role of mental disorder and crime and question whether some prisoners should in fact be in treatment It is widely agreed that many prisoners suffer with mental illness and psychological fragility. One must be mindful of the fact that the Equality

Act of 2010, and similar laws preceding this legislation, stipulate that the mentally disabled must not suffer any discrimination whatsoever.

There is a link between psychotic illness and violent crime. However not all violent criminals end up in Broadmoor and therefore they may end up in mainstream prisons. Many of these prisoners could possibly be cured of their violence with the appropriate anti psychotic medication. Therefore it is plausible to suggest that a course of psychiatric treatment might be a better option for some prisoners who should not really be in prison since they are mentally unwell.

It is sometimes observed that some sections of the mentally ill population have a propensity towards violence. However the prevalence of violence is ubiquitous in our society. Indeed “nature red in tooth and claw” is an accepted truism of the animal kingdom of which we are undoubtedly a part. The doctrine of “survival of the fittest” dictates that the aggressive hunter will bring home the bacon while the timid and timorous will starve to death. Therefore mankind undoubtedly evolved to be an ingenious as well as a vicious enemy.

That healthy and strong specimens of all species are aggressive predators is an accepted truism. However, most of us belonging to the Homo sapiens species endeavour to keep the baser instincts in check via exercising gargantuan self control! This is no mean feat as we are hard wired for aggression.

Our brains contain neural structures such as the limbic system and hippocampus that elicit aggressive behaviour when stimulated. Sometimes these structures become abnormally stimulated as a result of an organic pathology. For example let us take the case of a homicidal killing spree where the crazed perpetrator finally shot himself with his weapon. An autopsy found a massive brain tumour in the limbic system. This interesting case indicates how an organic malfunction of the brain may lead to violent acts.

If the limbic system was not wired for aggression then the irritating tumour may have elicited other strange behaviour. An organic pathology of the brain known as Capgras Syndrome, may result in the belief that a loved one is an imposter masquerading as a real person. This once caused a sufferer to murder the "robot that is pretending to be my Mother"! Capgras syndrome is caused by damage to the right hemisphere, possibly as a result of a stroke or epilepsy. Many strange behavioural syndromes may be caused by damage to the delicate brain .

Other cases of explosive violence have occurred after ingestion of red wine containing congeners and histamines. There is no doubt that a strong link exists between alcohol consumption and violence. This is partly due to the disinhibitory effect of alcohol on the brain. This ties in neatly with our previous assertion that our baser impulses need to be constantly reined in by our executive command which is situated in the prefrontal lobes.

The prefrontal lobes are essential for forward planning and self control. Damage to these areas, following a traffic accident, may result in impulsive and aggressive behaviour. Any brain damage can result in personality changes that may lead to violence or even homicidal hypersexuality.

Drinking alcohol depresses neural activity in the reasoning cerebral cortex with the result that latent lurking tendencies to violence are unleashed. Certain people also have a genetic intolerance to alcohol which means that they are unable to metabolise it in their liver. They may also have a mutation of the liver enzyme aldehyde dehydrogenase. This defect is very common in Chinese and Japanese people who may turn bright red if they consume alcohol.
Others may react to alcohol by becoming excessively violent and have no recollection whatsoever of their behaviour. We do not tend to call lager louts mentally disordered yet their behaviour clearly represents a risk to the public. The Saturday night is great for a fight ethos may lead

to serious injuries, and much violence occurs as a consequence of inebriation.

Following the same line of enquiry of substance misuse, there is a danger that certain drugs may elicit violent behaviour. Stimulants such as cocaine may leave the user vey paranoid. Other legal highs such as the bath salt Ivory Wave may lead to a paranoid psychosis. The new super strength Skunk may leave smokers feeling very paranoid owing to the high levels of tetrahydrocannabinol (THC).This type of strong cannabis has been bred via genetic modification of seeds. Many of these recreational drugs raise levels of the brain neuro transmitter dopamine. Dopamine levels have been correlated with pleasure. For instance, a strong cup of coffee will raise dopamine levels as does gambling and sex.

However, excess dopamine may cause pleasure to become paranoia. The phenothiazine drugs used to treat schizophrenia work by lowering brain levels of dopamine. Heavy skunk smokers may experience paranoid psychosis and imagine that people are talking about them behind their backs. A chef high on skunk stabbed Abigail Witchells in the back of the neck leaving her to bring up her children in a wheel chair. A paranoid person may feel that people are mocking him or even following him.

The paranoid delusions may become all encompassing and this is when a dangerous scenario may emerge. Paranoia is clearly correlated with the aetiology of violence. A label of paranoid schizophrenia may be given by a forensic psychiatrist or the person may escape unlabelled if the episode is a transitory one.

The whole issue of labelling mental illness is a large and possibly vexatious one that has been discussed by numerous psychologists . There was also an interesting study whereby psychiatrists pretended to be insane and hallucinating and were admitted to hospital. Once inside they behaved normally yet the staff refused to release them or recognise that they were "cured" of their psychosis!

Notwithstanding the difficulties of constructing mental illness it is an indisputable fact that paranoia is the flip side of aggression and is a worrying forensic symptom. Indeed Sigmund Freud wrote that paranoia was the projection outwards of a person` s inner base instincts. He called this murky subconscious repository of evil the ID.
So, for example, a person who did not like his mother in law might imagine that she hates him. Freud felt that the dislike of the relative had become projected out and then turned back against the perpetrator. So when we dislike someone we automatically deduce that this person *does not like us.* This is a simple explanation of the mechanics of paranoid thinking. It is therefore easy to understand how paranoia may lead to unpleasant acts being carried out to redress the imagined slights and insults.

It is well known that taking anabolic steroids may result in a paranoid syndrome known as Roid Rage (British Medical Journal). Men take steroids to bulk up their physique. However the steroids also induce rage and paranoia. The recent case of Raoul Moat illustrates the dangers of anabolic steroids. Moat was very fond of taking steroids to hone his masculine physique. He managed to continue taking them while in prison.
While in prison he heard that his girlfriend was dating a supposed policeman. Fuelled with a paranoid Roid rage he plotted revenge and as soon as he was released he embarked on a killing spree. One may speculate that had Moat not been taking steroids the tragic events might never have unfolded. Anabolic steroids taken to bulk up muscle are based on testosterone which is nature` s own hunting and killing hormone.

It has been reported that there is a culture of steroid use in the Welsh valleys by narcissistic young men keen to look fetching. This desire to be

real men may have resulted in the reported street brawls that have been gracing the pages of the popular press in South Wales recently.
The symptom of paranoia is therefore one to be taken extremely seriously by a mental health professional. It is arguably a very salient red flag warning of future violence. A paranoid person is not usually amenable to reason either. If a paranoid person imagines that others are plotting to kill him then he may decide to launch a pre-emptive strike to protect himself.

The paranoid person may think that the person who is following him is intent on harm. A whole set of elaborate and interconnected delusions may be constructed around the delusions of persecution. If he is a patient in a hospital he may suspect that the staff members are out to get him. This scenario has resulted in mental hospital staff sometimes tragically being murdered.
Paranoia is an extremely dangerous warning sign, yet it is often ignored. Sometimes patients have indicated that they are experiencing paranoid urges of violence to their psychiatrist and they are inexplicably gaily sent on their way to the outside world. They are then free to commit heinous and barbaric acts as they attempt to eliminate the perceived threats.

Sometimes the paranoia takes the form of voices that encourage wicked deeds. The Yorkshire ripper, Peter Sutcliffe, heard compelling voices telling him to rid the world of prostitutes. It has been speculated that such voices are the result of the inner articulations that are made when one thinks to oneself. In other words these voices are the very own thoughts that have been amplified by unknown neural processes. Thus the Yorkshire ripper spoke angrily to himself and believed that his thoughts were extraneous.

There have been numerous murders committed as a result of hearing commanding voices and this schizophrenic symptom must always be taken seriously. It is possible that raised dopamine facilitates this process of hearing one`s own thoughts aloud. Thus I would originally argue that paranoid schizophrenia as opposed to hebephrenic or silly schizophrenias is the most dangerous form of schizophrenia.

Another precursor of violence may be raised levels of depressive cortisol that is brought on by situations of "helplessness" as described by Seligman. In these cases normally loving Fathers may irrationally murder their children as the cortisol causes a deep and irrational fatalistic despair.

The Diagnostic and Statistical Manual has a whole list of mental disorders and categories to define the mentally disordered. The manual is constantly being changed and updated in line with the current zeitgeist. It seems that the manual has now become so all encompassing that we are all in danger of finding a description of ourselves in it. If I very much like the sound of my own ideas and pearls of wisdom does that mean I am a histrionic attention seeking narcissist? When does my desire for a spotlessly clean house become an ominous sign of obsessive compulsive disorder?

If I am afraid that my friends will desert me does that indicate a possible needy border line personality disorder? Just as the hypochondriac reading a medical book will start to imagine that he has every symptom so it is easy to be seduced by the fascinating range of symptoms in the DSM 1V. Indeed one may speculate that the only persons to escape a diagnostic label are the authors of such manuals!

The label of DSPD, dangerous, severe personality disorder has recently fallen out of fashion. The DSPD label has been hotly debated in the context of whether it is amenable to treatment. If someone is considered untreatable then there is no ground to detain that person in a mental institution. The whole area of civil liberties of the detention of the unwell was brought into the public arena by the Baxstrom Judgement of 1966.

The case set a judicial precedent which facilitated the release of a thousand unlawfully detained inmates from hospitals for the criminally insane in New York. Interestingly there was not widespread carnage or violence as many of the detainees quietly reintegrated back into the community. This example makes one question the skills of some mental health experts as well as the propensity to label deviant offenders as criminally insane.

Another category of offenders that may be prone to violence are those who lack fear or remorse. The term psychopath has been used to describe a constellation of traits that include callousness, egotism and lack of empathy. Recently the terms antisocial and dissocial personality have also been used to categorise those with a callous disregard for others. It has been speculated that there is an evolutionary niche for such ruthless behaviour and hence we see these latent psychopaths in the guise of successful bankers, politicians and businessmen.

This type of person may possibly be inclined to ruthless and violent behaviour towards those who cross their path and attempt to thwart their ambitions. The MacArthur actuarial study found a high correlation between this type of antisocial personality and violent acts. The sociopath does not suffer hallucinations and generally has not lost touch with reality. He is cool and calculating and shows no fear. Indeed he may be cortically under aroused or have an abnormal amygdala which prevents him feeling fear. Therefore he or she is not technically insane according to diagnostic criteria.

However this is a type of amoral insanity that can lead to dangerous and heartless behaviour. A sociopath running a business may cut corners and endanger the lives of others. If an offender suffers from a dissocial disorder as well as a psychotic illness then the results may be catastrophic. This co-morbidity of traits presents a serious threat to the public and such offenders need to be kept secure.

Let us examine the question of how the mentally disordered might also become the victims of violence. Those who are of a very low I.Q. and substantial learning disabilities may present an attractive opportunity for exploitation by amoral sociopaths or even normal people. Just as playground children are sometimes drawn to bully the weak and vulnerable so do adults sometimes maltreat those in need of most protection.

The feeble minded may unquestioningly obey orders that may endanger their lives and even embark on suicide terrorist missions if told to do so. Causing fires, as in explosions is also part of the MacDonald triad. It has been noted that some DSPD offenders have a triad of behaviours that includes a fascination with setting fires and childhood cruelty to animals. This is known as the MacDonald triad and has been used to predict sociopathic behaviour by criminologists.

The desire to cause explosions via terrorist acts could be considered as a manifestation of this fire starting sociopathic behaviour
Other cases of abuse may arise when a depressed person antagonises their spouse or partner with their constant moaning and groaning. This may cause the spouse to lose patience and lash out. Domestic abuse is very widespread and the neurotic partner may bring out latent hostility in their husband if they are depressed.

The condition of senile dementia or Alzheimer` s disease may also lead to geriatric abuse by family or professional carers . There have been numerous scandals involving abuse of elderly patients in care homes by their supposed nurses. This condition can make the sufferer behave in an extremely exasperating manner and therefore poses a real challenge to the carers. Some of the carers have lost patience and slapped their patients. It is often the case that those in a position of power or authority may be tempted to abuse that power.

This finding was demonstrated by the infamous American Prison experiment conducted in Stanford University. The pretend student prison guards behaved in such a bullying manner to the fake prisoners that the experiment had to be halted. People are easily corrupted by power and this has important implications for the weak and vulnerable in our society. Any person who is suffering from a mental disorder is therefore vulnerable to exploitation and even violence. A balance therefore needs to be struck between protecting the public and respecting the human rights and civil liberties of the patient.

Chapter Seven: Rough Justice?

When considering the role of prison it is important to remind ourselves that there have been many miscarriages of justice whereby innocent people have been incarcerated. Sometimes they have been framed or perhaps the Judge did not like the colour of their skin. Sometimes a person is convicted on hearsay or anecdotal evidence. It may take years before the truth emerges and the prisoner is finally freed. This is a salient reason for the moderation of the use of incarceration. Even worse is the scenario of an innocent prisoner being sent to Death Row.

Amanda Knox Case:

As a postgraduate criminologist I have recently been looking into gendered justice and the differential treatment often meted out to women who are portrayed as doubly deviant by a patriarchal sentencing culture. Sometimes women are sexualised in a babes behind bars fashion and given such huge coverage by a media keen to sell newspapers that their trial becomes seriously prejudiced .

This scenario occurred in the Amanda`s Knox case which degenerated into a witch hunt. It suits a lot of people to believe that she was guilty since a lot of money has been made out of her as a media subject. Her trial in Italy was completely prejudiced. A cartoon in the press had already appeared showing the murder with three people present before her trial.

I believed that she was totally innocent for numerous reasons, not least the forensic evidence which completely removes her from the crime scene. Her case was badly presented the first time, focussing on emotional appeals to the judge instead of presenting the hard facts.

Some of these facts are as follows:

1. The main suspect ,Rudy Guede had recently been apprehended twice armed with a knife having broken into a school and an office to steal laptops.

2. Guede gained entrance on both occasions via a window he had smashed with a rock.

3.In the Knox case a window was similarly smashed with a rock in an adjacent room to Meredith`s room.

4. The Italian Judge decided that this was a "staged break in" by Knox and Sollecito.

5.A criminologist would think otherwise. This clearly was a genuine break in by a drug dealer looking for money.

6.The Italian Judge says the motive for murder is baffling but probably has sexual satanic undertones.

7. Wrong again; there is a clear motive of THEFT as Rudy Guede left his fingerprints on Meredith`s handbag and also stole 300 Euros from it.

8. At around 10 o clock in the evening Meredith noticed the missing money and tried to phone her bank .(evidence found on her phone records). Guede is in the bathroom at this point using the lavatory (evidence later found).

9. Between 10 and 11 pm. Meredith Kercher is murdered and raped, by Rudy Guede.

10. He takes her mobile phones and throws them in a neighbour`s garden where they are later found.

11.He then runs away to Germany: another indication of guilt.

12.He says in his police statement that he left the front door open

13. Amanda Knox states that when she arrived at the murder house the front door was wide open, arousing her suspicions.

14,Amanda hardly knew Guede and could not have conferred with him. Therefore she is telling the truth about the wide open door.

15. Meredith`s door was locked from the outside by the killer and therefore these keys need to be found as they will provide crucial DNA evidence.

16. Guede said that he had consensual sex with Meredith on a date arranged previously at the Halloween party. Witnesses said he was not at the Halloween party and did not meet Meredith. It was clearly a rape.

17. Guede stated that he returned to the room to find Sollecito stabbing Meredith. This is clearly an amateurish attempt to frame another man for his heinous crime. Amazingly the prosecution fell for this shabby lie resulting in Sollecito`s arrest.

18. If Guede`s story is true why did he not call an ambulance??

To conclude, two innocent people were wrongly incarcerated and received longer sentences than the real culprit who is only serving sixteen years. Let us not underestimate the extent of police corruption especially in countries such as Italy. The prosecutor was a bit of a bully and later he himself was convicted of a charge pertaining to an abuse of office in another criminal case. Poor Amanda was beaten on the head and interrogated all night long without a lawyer present. Then she was forced to sign a confession or a statement by the bullying police.

I wrote this to the Italian Court of Appeal at the time of the new sentencing. Fortunately one of my Italian Mother`s relatives was a highly respected High Court Judge and so I took the opportunity to mention this in my letter that I had written in my very best Italian!
I felt very strongly that a terrible miscarriage of justice had taken place. It was a relief to all concerned when both Amanda Knox and Rafael Sollecito were released.

There was not a shred of DNA evidence to implicate either of the two young students. The crime scene was also badly contaminated with the inept police moving the evidence and traipsing around.

It is often the case that police corruption is endemic within the criminal justice system. In this case the prosecutor was highly imaginative and had conjured up a very lurid picture of an imaginary sex game. The prosecutor was a very intimidating figure who had previously intimidated a journalist over his written theories of the famous murders in Florence.

The poor journalist nearly ended up being accused of being the infamous murdering monster of Florence! This is because the imagination of Prosecutor Mignini simply knows no bounds. The Prosecutor, Giuliano Mignini, also was charged with corruption. He allegedly consulted a fortune teller prior to the notorious "Foxy

Knoxy" trial. The crystal ball told him that the murder was a sex game gone wrong. Such flimsy supernatural evidence should not have influenced due process in a Court of Law.

Rough Justice: Bamber Cafell

The Bamber Cafell case continues to fascinate detectives. The murder of two twin children, their young mother and their grandparents took place on an isolated farm in the year 1986. It was widely deduced that Bamber had wiped out his entire family in order to secure an inheritance of the farm and cottage.
However the evidence of the crime scene was contaminated by hordes of inept police officers trampling through the crime scene. Therefore one can never be wholly sure that Bamber Cafel was indeed the perpetrator of this heinous crime.

His sister was a pretty model known as Bambi Cafell. She also had a history of mental illness and t is entirely possible that it was she who committed the murders of her family and then turned the gun on herself to commit suicide. Why would she have done such a thing? Well her adoptive parents were nagging her a lot and there had been some terrible arguments at the farm cottage.

The step parents had then threatened to take the twins away from Bambi and to get custody over them. This pan had caused Bambi to erupt into a psychotic rage. One has to remember that she had already been diagnosed with a psychotic illness.

People with some forms of paranoid psychosis can become quite violent. It is therefore feasible that upon hearing of the pans to take her twin boys away from her that the unstable young mother just flipped. She grabbed the gun and a struggle ensued. There was evidence of a struggle at the scene.

This case portrays the Criminal Justice System in a most inefficient and inept light. The crime scene was disturbed by hordes of marauding police officers . The police even allowed a firearms training unit to enter the murder crime to conduct a training exercise using the corpses.

The murder weapon and murdered bodies were moved around as clearly evidenced by the photographs.
Initially the murder was held to be a tragic consequence of a Mother who had gone beserk and killed her own children and parents before killing herself. Subsequently the brother was convicted of the murder on the hearsay of a bitter ex- girlfriend who was nursing a grievance against Bamber Cafell.

As the stepfather was being attacked by an enraged step daughter he managed to get to his phone and he called Bmber to come and help saying that his sister had gone crazy and was trying to shoot everyone. The elderly man had managed to wrestle the gun form her hands.

By the time that Bamber had arrived at White House Farm which is in Tolleshunt D ` Arcy, Essex, the entire family had been wiped out. Since the sister Bambi was no longer alive she could not be questioned properly by detectives.

The sister had been diagnosed with paranoid schizophrenia which is a condition associated with very dangerous and violent behaviour. Bambi Cafell had also recently decided to stop taking her anti psychotic medication that was needed to keep her moods calm and stable. All of this medical evidence I find to be very compelling to make a case that she was perpetrator of this heinous crime.

The angry girlfriend who was called Julie Mugford told police that her former boyfriend had often said that he wanted to kill his family and to

collect a substantial inheritance. One has to ask oneself just how plausible this statement really is.
If a person is intending to commit mass murder in order to collect a vast sum of money would they really be so very foolish as to broadcast their cunning plan to all and sundry??

Surely not even the most naive and hopeless of criminals would not be so foolish as to let the cat out of the bag about a heinous crime that they are planning to commit.
Frankly the whole sounds exceedingly suspect and fishy!
Even more suspicious is the fact that the bitter girlfriend then sold her story to the News of The World Newspaper for £25, 000 which was an absolute fortune back in 1985.

The bitter scorned girlfriend said that her ex boyfriend killed his entire family and he did it to get the inheritance of White House Farm. The prosecution star witness was herself involved in a fraud previously to do with cheques but this fact of her character was conveniently kept secret in the court proceedings.

Indeed the attractive farm and its cottages was a very nice place to own. However we have to ask ourselves why a girlfriend would shop a former boyfriend in this way. It seems that revenge was a motive since she had been dumped in a most thoughtless manner.
As the saying goes" revenge has no fury like a woman scorned!!

Then a couple of greedy cousins also emerged to deliver the final nail in Bamber`s coffin. These cousins stood to inherit the valuable farm but only when the main contender was put safely behind bars!
Therefore the cousins then sided with the revengeful girlfriend. Together the three of them then proceeded to deliver a damning character assassination of Bamber Cafell.

The defendant was portrayed as a greedy mercenary man who had murdered his family to secure an early inheritance. Perhaps he should not have ditched his girlfriend. The evidence on which Bamber was convicted centred around the gun silencer which had allegedly got the blood of Bambi on it but was found in a cupboard. The logic says that if she killed everyone and then herself then she could not have put the silencer back in the cupboard.

However once again the evidence is flawed since it was one of the greedy cousins who happened to conveniently find the allegedly blood stained silencer and then it emerged that the police never ran any checks to see who the blood actually belonged to. You have to remember that this was back in the decade of the 80`s when forensic science was not nearly as advanced as it is today. Therefore the crime scene evidence was not very compelling and it had also been tampered with.

Bamber Cafell has continued to maintain his innocence but he has been ignored and the Court of Appeal seem to have made up their minds that he is a most wicked killer.
He has been given a whole life tariff that is usually reserved for the most evil of criminals. However the facts of the matter are that most if not all of the evidence is very circumstantial and that three people have made a lot of money by the fact that Bamber is safely behind bars. The cousins inherited the valuable farmhouse and the former girlfriend was paid handsomely for her story.
In my opinion this is a possible case of rough justice.

Nowadays there is sophisticated software known as voice recognition analysis that can detect if a person is lying. This VRA software is used by actuarial insurance assessors. This girlfriend`s statement needs to be placed under such scientific scrutiny to ascertain its veracity. This has not been done and therefore the statement amounts to no more than hearsay. As evidence it is therefore worthless. It seems that Bamber Cafell has been convicted purely because the jury and Judge did not like the look of him.

This is known as the negative halo effect. If a jury likes the look of the defendant then there can be a positive halo effect which results in a better outcome. In Bamber`s case the jury had already made their mind up that he was a shady character and therefore he must be guilty.

Members of the jury are ordinary people with their tendency towards bias either for or against a defendant. The emotional nature of judgements is of great concern. A judgement should be based purely on the facts and the evidence. However psychological studies have proven that an impartial and fact based judgement is not always guaranteed in a court of law. The jury may be swayed even by the appearance of the defendant. A study even found that attractive women were more likely to get a lighter sentence!

If the defendant has been subjected to weeks of a character assassination by a hungry press then it is very difficult for that person to receive an impartial and a fair trial.

The sister known as Bambi Cafell suffered with paranoid schizophrenia. It is very common for sufferers of this disorder to commit violent or murderous acts. The list is vast. There have been many documented cases.

A paranoid mother named Theresa Riggi was convicted of stabbing her three children to death in an argument over custody with her estranged partner. The custody proceedings had pushed her over the edge and into a temporary insanity.

A paranoid father also tried to kill his children by driving into a river after an argument with his ex partner. Another father jumped from a hotel balcony with his two children after rowing with his wife. The list of children murdered by insane and temporarily insane parents is sadly a lengthy one.

Often it is a temporary episode of extreme madness and the parent will later have to live with the consequences for the rest of their pitiful lives. Many of these murdering parents have simply flipped and most certainly do love their children. Sometimes the children are murdered out of a twisted desire for revenge against the partner. Because there are such a large number of cases of infanticide caused by custody proceedings one has to at least consider that this might have happened in the infamous farm murders.

On the night of the killings, there had been an argument between the Mother Bambi Cafell and her foster parents about the children. Arguments about children have been shown to be a trigger for irrational and murderous behaviour towards infants. Bambi may have been driven to a precipice of homicidal insanity by the inflammatory comments.

This would have been exacerbated by the time of the dispute. It was very late and she would have been over tired and irritable. Being of a paranoid nature she would not take criticism well.
The conclusion of this analysis is that the Appeal Court has been negligent. They have made a judgement based on prejudice and stereotypy. And may have put an innocent man behind bars for life.

A similar scenario has occurred with poor Amanda Knox who is bore her trial with great fortitude. The trial was one of a character assassination whereby she was called Foxy Knoxy with the implication that she was a foxy type of girl. The press seemed to make the unfair innuendo that a foxy lady would like to indulge in kinky past times. Her trial was completely prejudiced by the lurid press coverage. It would have been impossible for the jury not to have read the front page headlines. It was hardly surprising then that the young student was initially found guilty.

Anyone who still harbours the slightest suspicions should remind themselves that police corruption can seriously distort the evidence that is provided before a court of law. It is also statistically very rare for women to murder just for kicks and for sexual thrills as the deranged prosecutor Giuliano Mignini had alleged. Without doubt Amanda Knox was framed and was a victim of a terrible miscarriage of justice.

Conclusion:

There is often a desire for retribution when a shocking crime is committed. When a loved one is stabbed or when innocent children are killed by dangerous drivers, feelings run high and there is a demand for tough and long sentences. Punishing sentences help to fulfil an understandable desire for retribution and revenge.
The culture of retribution reaches its absolute zenith in American supermax prisons. Some of the toughest prison sentences are also handed down in American Courts of Law where sentences of hundreds of years are not uncommon! This punitive approach is often needed where heinous crimes are committed that appal and outrage the public. However in many cases prison simply does m=not work well for society and many prisoners exit prison with a drug problem acquired in prison and other criminal habits learnt from their fellow inmates.

References:

Chapter One:

Ardrey,R. (1966) *the Territorial Imperative*. New York: Dell
Babiak,P. and Hare ,R.D.(2006), *Snakes in Suits: When Psychopaths Go To Work*, New York: Harper Collins.
BBC News 2002, Business, "Did Enron Manipulate Energy Crisis"http://news.bbc.co.uk/1/hi/business/1972574.stm accessed 2011-02-07

BBC News (Feb. 12 2008) Mosquito Device Divides Opinion"http://news.bbc.co.uk/1/hi/uk/7240653.stmaccessed 2011-03-07

BBC News (Jan.30 2011) CS Spray Used on UK UNCUT Protest http://www.bbc.co.uk/news/uk-england-12318896Protest accessed 2011-02-06

Baker, S. P. (2009) "Trends in Unintentional Injury Deaths" *American Journal of Preventive Medicine,* volume 37, issue 3, pages 188-194.

Bialik, C. (2010) "Dubious Origins for Drugs, and Stats about Them" *The Numbers Guy, Wall Street Journal September 10 2010*

Box, S. (1983) *Power, Crime and Mystification*, London: Tavistock.

Braithwaite, J. (1984), *Corporate Crime in the Pharmaceutical Industry*, London: Routledge & Kegan Paul.

Buss, D. M. (2005) *the Murderer next door: Why the Mind is Designed to Kill,* New York: Penguin Press.

Chambliss, (1975) Towards a Political Economy of Crime, *Theory and Society,* March, 149-170.

Christie, N. (2004) *a Suitable Amount of Crime*, London: Routledge.

Clarke, R.V. and Felson, M. (1993) "Introduction: Criminology, Routine Activity and rational Choice" *Advances in Theoretical Criminology: Routine Activity and Rational Choice:* vol. 5 pp. 1-14

Cleckley, H. (1977) *The Mask of Sanity* 5th edition, St. Louis: Mosby.

Cohen, L.E. and Felson, M. (1979) "Social Change and Crime Rate Trends, a Routine Activity Approach" *American Sociological Review,* 44 (4) pp. 588-608.

Darwin, C. (1872a) *The Origin of Species*, New York: Macmillan, 6th edition, 1962

Dawkins, R. (1989) *the Selfish Gene*, Oxford, OUP.

Dobash, R.E., and Dobash, R. D (1979)*Violence against Wives*, New York; Free Press.

Dobash, R.E. and Dobash, R.D. (1992) *Women, Violence and social change*, London; Routledge.

Felson, M. (1994) *Crime and Everyday Life; Insight and Implications for Society*. Thousands Oaks: Pine Forge Press.

Garland, D. (2008) "On the Concept of Moral Panic", *Crime, Media, Culture,* 4: 9-30.

Goswami, N. (2011) "SFO Must Swallow its Medicine After Falling Short in its NHS Price-Fixing Case". *The Lawyer*, January 11 2011http://www.thelawyer.com/sfo-must-swallow-its-medicine-after-falling-short-in-nhs-price-fixing-case/133899.article accessed 2011-01-10

Gottfredson, M. R. and Hirschi, T. (1990) *A General Theory of Crime*, Stanford CA: Stanford University Press.

Greenwood , C. (2010) "Organised Crime Gangs Outwitting Police" The Independent July 13 2010. http://www.independent.co.uk/news/uk/crime/organised-crime-gangs-outwitting-police-2025348.html accessed v2011-01-12

Hare, R. D.(1993) *Without Conscience: the Disturbing World of Psychopaths Among Us*, New York : Pocket Books.

Hare, R. D.(2003) *Manual for the Revised Psychopathy Checklist* (2nd edition) Toronto, Canada Multi Health Systems.

Institute of Fiscal Studies (IFS) (21 October 2010) "Spending Review Cuts hit Poor Hardest", says Institute of Fiscal Studies, http://www.u.tv/news/Spending-review-cuts-hit-poor-hardest-says-Institute-of-Fiscal-Studies/96cdbe23-3770-47f3-94f9-a1697ebf9b03s accessed 2011-03-06

MacPherson, W. (1999) Stephen Lawrence Inquiry, London: HMSO

Marx, K. and Engels, F. (1848) *Manifesto of the Communist Party*, in Marx-Engels Selected Works London: Lawrence and Wishart.

Marx, K. (1904) originally published (1859)*Critique of Political Economy,* New York: International Library.

Ministry of Justice (2008/09) Statistics on Race and the Criminal Justice System 2008/09, a Ministry of justice Publication under Section 95 of the Criminal Justice Act 1991.

Nelken, D. (2007), *White-Collar and Corporate Crime: 4th Edition*. Chapter 22, *The Oxford Handbook of Criminology*, edited by Mike Maguire, Rod Morgan, and Robert Reiner, Oxford: Oxford University Press.
Phillips, C. (2010) 'Institutional Racism and Ethnic Inequalities: An Expanded Multilevel Framework', *Journal of Social Policy*
Poundstone, W. (1992*) Prisoners Dilemma*, New York: Doubleday.
Pruitt, D. (1971) Choice shifts in group discussion: An introductory review. *Journal of Personality and Social Psychology, 20*(3), 339-360
Punch, M. (1996) *Dirty Business, Exploring Corporate Misconduct: Analysis and Cases*, London: Sage Publications Ltd.
Reiman, J. (1984) *the Rich Get Richer and the Poor Get Prison*, New York: Macmillan
Sellin, T. (1938*) Culture Conflict and Crime*, New York: Social Science Research Council.
Slapper, G and Tombs, A S. (1999) *Corporate Crime*, Harlow: Longman.
Smith, R.,and Sidal, R. (Sep. 27 2010) "Banks Keep Failing, No End In sight" *Wall Street Journal*, Business Section.
Sutherland, E. (1937) *the Professional Thief*, Chicago: University of Chicago Press.
Sutherland, E. (1949;1983) *White Collar Crime: The Uncut Version*, New Haven: Yale University Press.
UK Police Online (Oct.16 2010) "Anger over Return of Sus Laws that will let Police target minorities",http://www.ukpoliceonline.co.uk/index.php?/topic/43554-sus-laws/ accessed
WHO (2009) World Health Organisation : Media Centre Medicines : Counterfeit Medicines. Factsheet No. 275.
Young, J. (1999) *the Exclusive Society? Social exclusion, crime and difference in Late*

modernity, London: Sage.

Chapter Two: Equality, Diversity and Criminal Justice

Allen, H. (1987) *Justice Unbalanced*, Buckingham; Open University Press.
Allport, g. (1958*) The Nature of Prejudice,* NY Doubleday, Anchor Books.

Becker, H. S. (1963) *Outsiders: Studies in the Sociology of Deviance,* New York: Free Press

Bohn, R. M. (1997) *A Primer on Crime and Delinquency,*Belmont, CA: Wadsworth.
Bottoms, A.E. and McWilliams, W. (1979) "A Non-Treatment Paradigm for Probation Practice", *British Journal of Social Work,* 9, 2, pp. 159-202

Bottoms, A. (1995) "The Philosophy and Politics of Punishment and Sentencing", in Clarkson. C. and Morgan, R. (eds) *The Politics of sentencing Reform*, Oxford, Clarendon Press.
Bowling, B., and Phillips, C. (2002) Racism, Crime and Justice, Harrow, UK: Longman.
Box, S. (198 *Power, Crime and Mystification* ,London: Tavistock.
Braithwaite J. (1989*) Crime, Shame and Reintegration*, Cambridge: Cambridge University Press.
Brathwaite, J. Ahmed,E. Harris, N. Brathwaite, V. (2001) *Shame Management Through Reintegration*, Melbourne: Cambridge University Press.
Burnett, R. and Eaton, G. (2004) "Factors Associated with Effective Practice in Approved Premises" Home Office Online report 65/04.

Calverley, A. Cole, B. Kaur, G., Lewis, S. Raynor, P. Sadeghi, S. Smith, Vanstone, M. (2004)"Black and Asian Offenders on Probation", Home Office Research Study, 277, London: Home Office.
Carlen, P. and Tchaikovsky, C. (1996) "Women` s Imprisonment in England and Wales at the End of the Century: Legitimacy, Realities and Utopias." Chapter.10 in Matthews, R. and Francis,

P.(eds.) *Prisons 2000: An International Perspective on the Present state and future of Imprisonment.* Basingstoke: Macmillan.
Carlen, P. (2002) *Women and Punishment; the Struggle for Justice* Cullompton: Willan.

Cherry, S. (2005; 2010) *Transforming Behaviour: Pro social Modelling In Practice,* Cullompton: Willan.

Cohen, S. (1973) *Folk devils and Moral Panics: the Creation of Mods and Rockers,* London: Martin Robertson

Corston, Baroness,Jean (13 March 2007) Women in the Criminal Justice System. , the Corston Report in *the Howard Journal of Criminal Justice.*
Dobash, R.E. and Dobash, R. D (1979) *Violence against Wives*, New York; Free Press.
Dodd, V. "The Missed danger signals that led to a Brutal Murder" the Guardian, Friday 30 June 2006.
Dowden, C. and Andrews, D.A. (1999) "What Works for Female Offenders: A Meta-Analytic Review", *Crime and Delinquency*, vol.45 no.4 pp.438-452.
Fawcett Society (2009) Engendering Justice-from policy to practice; Final Report of the Commission ; Women and the Criminal Justice System, London; *Fawcett Society.*
Gard, R. (2007) "The First Probation Officers in England and Wales 1906=14", *British Journal of Criminology* 47, 6, pp. 938-954.
Garland, D. (2008) "On the Concept of Moral Panic", *Crime, Media, Culture,* 4: 9-30.
Gelsthorpe, L. (2001) Accountability: Difference and Diversity in the Deliverance of Community Penalties in A. Bottoms, L. Gelsthorpe and S. Rex (eds) *Community penalties: Change and Challenges*: Cullompton: Willan.
Gelsthorpe, L. and Worrall, A. (2009) "Looking for Trouble: a Recent History of Girls, Young Women and Youth Justice", *Youth Justice December 2009 vol. 9 no. 3 209-223*
Gordon, D. & Pantazis, C. (1997) *Breadline Britain in the 1990s.* Aldershot: Ashgate Publishing
Hedderman, C. and Hough, M. (1994) "Does the Criminal justice System

Treat Men and Women Differently"? Home Office Research and Statistics Department, Research Findings No. 10, Research and Planning Unit.
Her Majesty` s Inspectorate of Probation (2000) "Towards Race Equality", London: Home Office.
Hillyard, P. (with C. Pantazis, S. Tombs and D. Gordon) (2004)*Beyond Criminology: Taking Harm Seriously*, Pluto Press
Hirschi. T. (1967*) Delinquency Research*, New York: The Free Press.
Hirschi, T. (1969) *Causes of Delinquency*, Berkeley and Los Angeles: University of California Press.
Hood, R. (1992) *Race and Sentencing in the Crown Court*, Oxford: Clarendon Press.
Hope, C. (31 March 2010) "Probation Officers tell JP` s to Stop Sending them Offenders because of Budget Constraints", Guardian Report
Home Office (1984 Probation service in England and Wales: Statement of National Objectives and Priorities, SNOP, London: Home Office.
Jarvis, F. (1972*) Advise, Assist and Befriend: a History of the Probation and After-Care Service,* London: NAPO.
Loucks, N., Malloch, M., McIvor, G., and Gelsthorpe, L. (2006)" Time-Out for Women: Innovation in Scotland in a Context of Change" *Howard Journal of Criminal Justice,* 29 Nov. 2007https://dspace.stir.ac.uk/dspace/bitstream/1893/1107/1/Howard%20Journal%20Nov%2007.pdf
MacPherson, W. (1999) Stephen Lawrence Inquiry, London: HMSO.
Martin, J., Kautt,P., and Gelsthorpe, L. (2009) "What Works for Women*", British Journal of Criminology*49, 879-899.
McGuire J. (2000*) Cognitive behavioural approaches; an introduction to theory and research*, London, HMIP
Merton, R.K. (1995) "The Thomas Theorem and the Matthew Effect" *Social Forces,* December 1995, 74(2):379-424
Messerschmidt, J. W. (1993*), Masculinities and Crime* .Lanham, MD; Rowman and Littlefield..
Messerschmidt, J.W. (2000) "Becoming real men; adolescent masculinity challenges and sexual violence", *Men & Masculinities*, 2 (3), pp.266-307.
Ministry of Justice (2008/09) Statistics on Race and the Criminal Justice System 2008/09, a Ministry of justice Publication under Section 95 of the Criminal Justice Act 1991.
Ministry of Justice (2010) Statistics on Women and the Criminal Justice

System: A Ministry of Justice Publication under Section 95 of the

Criminal Justice Act 1991.

Pantazis, C. & Gordon, D. (1996) "Television licence evasion and the criminalisation of female poverty". *Howard Journal of Criminal Justice*, 36, pp. 170-186.
Phillips, C. (2010) 'Institutional Racism and Ethnic Inequalities: An Expanded Multilevel Framework', *Journal of Social Policy*
Pitts, J. (2009) "Youth Gangs, Ethnicity, and the Politics of Estrangement", *Youth and Policy*. No. 102, Spring.
Punch, M. (1996) *Dirty Business, Exploring Corporate Misconduct: Analysis and Cases*, London: Sage Publications Ltd.
Raine, J.W. and. Willson, M.J. (1996) "Managerialism and beyond: the case of criminal justice", *International Journal of Public Sector Management,* Vol. 9: 4, pp.20 - 33
Raynor, P. and Vanstone, M. (1994) 'Probation Practice, Effectiveness and the Non-Treatment Paradigm', *British Journal of Social Work*, 24(4): 387-404.
Sentences, Mid Glamorgan Probation Service.
Raynor, P. and Vanstone, M. (2002) *Understanding Community Penalties,* Buckingham: Open University Press.
Raynor, P. (2007) "Community Penalties: Probation "What Works", and Offender Management" in the *Oxford Handbook of Criminology*, edited by Mike Maguire, Rod Morgan, and Robert Reiner, Oxford: Oxford university press.
Reiman, J. (1984) *the Rich Get Richer and the Poor Get Prison*, New York: Macmillan
Ross, R.R. and Fabiano, E.A. (1985) *Time to Think; a Cognitive Model of Delinquency Prevention and Offender Rehabilitation,*Johnson City, TN, Institute of Social Sciences and Arts.
Ross, R.R. and Fabiano, E.A. and Ross, R.D. (1986) *Reasoning and Rehabilitation: a Handbook for Teaching Cognitive Skills,*Ottawa: University of Ottawa.
Sellin, T. (1938) *Culture, Conflict and Crime*, New Jersey: Social Science Research Council.
Skinner, B.F. (16 April 1984). "The Operational analysis of psychological terms" *Behavioural and Brain Sciences,* **7** (4): 547–581.
Sutherland, E. (1937) *the Professional Thief*, Chicago: University of Chicago Press.
Sutherland, E. (1983) *White Collar Crime: The Uncut Version*, New Haven: Yale University Press.
Travis, A. (Thursday 8 July 2010) Guardian, "Anti-terror stop and search plans to be scrapped"http://www.guardian.co.uk/law/2010/jul/08/anti-terror-stop-and-search-scrapped
Turk, A. (1969) *Criminality and Legal Order*, Chicago: Rand McNally.
Zedner, L.(1991) *Women, Crime and Custody in Victorian England,* Oxford: Oxford University Press.

Chapter Three

Allen, H. (1987) *Justice Unbalanced*, Buckhingham; Open University Press
BBC News 13 October 2010 http://news.bbc.co.uk-11532241accessed 2010-12-11
BBC News Mid Wales 8 November 2010 "Anger over rape case jailing of Powys woman". http://www.BBC.co.uk/news/uk-wales-mid-wales-11707903.accessed 2010-12-10
Black, D. (1992) "Children of Parents in Prison", *Archives of Diseases in Childhood* 67:967-97.
Bohn, R. M. (1997) *A Primer on Crime and Delinquency,*. Belmont, CA ;Wadsworth.
Bosworth, M (2006) "Self-harm in women`s prisons" *Criminology*5: 157-159..
Bottoms, A. (1995) "The Philosophy and Politics of Punishment and Sentencing", in Clarkson. C. and Morgan, R. (eds) *The Politics of sentencing Reform*, Oxford, Clarendon Press.
Bowlby, J. (1969) *Attachment and Loss.*, Vol. 1 Attachment; New York; Basic Books.
Bowlby, J. (1973) *Attachment and Loss*, Vol. 2. Separation, New York ; Basic Books.
Carlen, P. (1983) *Women`s Imprisonment*. London ; Routledge and Kegan Paul.
Carlen, P. and Tchaikovsky, C. (1996) "Women`s Imprisonment in England and Wales at the End of the Century: Legitimacy, Realities and Utopias." Chapter.10 in Matthews, R. and Francis,

P.(eds.) *Prisons 2000: An International Perspective on the Present state and future of Imprisonment.* Basingstoke: Macmillan.
Carlen, P.(ed.) (2002), *Women and Punishment; The Struggle for Justice,* Cullompton ; Willan.,
Carlen, P. and Worrall, A (2006)"Analysing Women`s Imprisonment", Chapter 14 in
Chesney-Lind, M. (2006) Patriarchy, Crime and Justice, Feminist Criminology in an era of Backlash, *Feminist Criminology* (1); 6-26.
Cecil, D. K. (2007) "Doing Time in Camp Cupcake: Lessons learnt from Newspaper accounts of Martha Stewart`s Incarceration." *Journal of Criminal Justice and Popular Culture,*14 (2) 142-160.
CIVITAS Institute of the Study of Civil Society 2010 Factsheet-Prisons in England and Wales. http://www.civitas.org.uk/crime/factsheet-Prisons.pdf accessed 2010-12-10
CLINKS (2010 "Less Equal Than Others"http://www.clinks.org/publications/reports/r4j-report accessed 2010-12-11
Codd, H. (15 June2007) Prisoners Families and Resettlement; A Critical Analysis, *The Howard Journal of Criminal Justice*
Corston, Baroness, the Corston Report- 13 March 2007- Women in the Criminal Justice System. *The Howard Journal of Criminal Justice* .
Crook, F. The Guardian, 2 August 2006 , Close Down Women`s Prisons http://www.guardian.co.uk/commentisfree/2006/aug/02/closedownwomensprisons
Diamond Project, Wednesday 1 December Channel 4 News ;Met`s Diamond Project May Cut Reoffending and Save Money..channel4.com/news/net-police-rehabilitation-project-under-threat.
Dobash, R.E., and Dobash, R. D (1979) *Violence against Wives*, New York; Free Press.
Dobash, R.E. and Dobash, R.D.(1992) *Women, Violence and social change*, London; Routledge.
Dooley, E. (1990) Prison Suicide in England and Wales, 1972-87*British Journal of Psychiatry* 156, 40-45.
The Equality Act 1 October 2010 Government Equalities Office,http://www.equalities.gov.uk/equality_act_2010.aspx accessed 2010-12-10
Every Child Matters (2003) Green Paper http://www.dcsf.gov.uk/everychildmatters/about/aims/outcomes/outcomescyp/ accessed 2010-12-11
Fawcett Society (2009) Engendering Justice-from policy to practice; Final Report of the Commission ; women and the Criminal Justice System, London; Fawcett Society.
Freeman, S. *The mistake that cost Roy Meadows his reputation*; the Sunday Times Online, February 17 2006http://www.timesonline.co.uk/tol/news/uk/article731981.eceaccessed 2010-12-10
Harlow, H.F. (1958) The Nature of Love ; *American Psychologist* 13 673-85.
Harlow, H. F. and Zimmerman, R.R. (1959) Affectional Responses in the Infant Monkey. *Science* 130:421-32.
Hedderman, C. and Hough, M (1994) Does the Criminal Justice System Treat Men and Women Differently?, Home Office Research and Statistics Department, Research Findings No. 10, Research and Planning Unit.
Her Majesty`s Chief Inspectorate of Prisons, HMCIP (2000), An unannounced follow up Inspection of HM Prison Holloway, London; Home Office.
H.M. Prison Service (2010)http://www.hmprisonservice.gov.uk/resourcecentre/publicationsdocuments/index.asp?cat=85 accessed 2010-12-10
The Howard, Sentencing Statistics for England and Wales 2010.http://www.howardleague.org/1191/ accessed 2010-12-10
Jewkes,Y. and Johnston, H. (2007) "the Evolution of Prison Architecture" p.174-196 in Jewkes (ed) *Handbook on Prisons*, Cullompton: Willan.
Jones, S. (2008) Partners in Crime; a study of the relationship between the offenders and their co-defendants, *Criminology & Criminal Justice,* 8(2) pp147-64.
Katz, J. (1987), 'What Makes Crime "News"?, *Media, Culture and Society,* 9(1): 47-75

Liebling,A. and Morgan, R.(2007), Imprisonment ;An Expanding Scene, Chapter 32 in Oxford Handbook of Criminology 4th Edition, Edited by Mike Maguire, Rod Morgan, and Robert Reiner; Oxford University Press.
Loucks, N., Malloch, M., McIvor, G., and Gelsthorpe, L. (2005)" Time-Out for Women : Innovation in Scotland in a Context of Change
"https://dspace.stir.ac.uk/dspace/bitstream/1893/1107/1/Howard%20Journal%20Nov%2007.pdf accessed 2010-12-11
Messerschmidt, J. W.(1993*), Masculinities and Crime* .Lanham, MD; Rowman and Littlefield..
Messerschmidt, J.W.(2000) Becoming real men; adolescent masculinity challenges and sexual violence, *Men & Masculinities*, 2 (3), pp.266-307.

Chapter Four

Abramson, LY. Seligman, M. E.P .and Teasdale, J. D. (1978) "Learned helplessness in humans; Critique and reformulation."*Journal of Abnormal Psychology* 87; 49-74
Abramson, L. Y. Metalsky, G. L., and Alloy, I. B. (1989) Hopelessness Depression; a theory based subtype. *Psychological Review*, 96, 358-372.
ACTION for Prisoners Families -
AFP:http://www.actionforprisonersfamilies.org.uk/uploadedFiles/About_Us/APF%20Three%20Year%20Strategy%202009-12.pdfaccessed 2010-12-11
Ardrey, R (1966)*The Territorial imperative*. NewYork; Dell.
Audit Commission and the Wales Audit Office, (2006)" Crime Recording 2005: Improving the Quality of Crime Records in Police Authorities and Forces in England and Wales", London Audit Commission.
Bandura, Ross and Ross (1963) Imitation of film- mediated aggressive models. *Journal of Abnormal and Social Psychology*66:3-11
Bandura, A (1965) Influence of models `reinforcement contingencies on the acquisition of imitative responses.; *Journal of Personality and Social Psychology* :589-95
BBC News 9 July (2008) Haltemprice campaign nearing endhttp://news.bbc.co.uk/1/hi/uk_politics/7497290.stm, accessed 2010-12-11
BBC NEWS October 5 2010 "Prisoners must work a 40 hour Week says Ken Clarke." http://www.bbc.co.uk/news/uk-politics-11470289 accessed 2010-12-11
BBC News 13 October 2010 Proposals 'could mean 3,000 fewer' jailed for assault http://www.bbc.co.uk/news/uk-11532241, accessed 2010-12-11
Black, I, and Kamali, S. Tuesday 31 August (2010) Guardianhttp://www.guardian.co.uk/world/2010/aug/31/sakineh-mohammadi-ashtiani-mock-execution-stoning accessed 2010-12-11
Bloom .B & Steinhart .D (1993)" Why punish the children? A reappraisal of the children of incarcerated Mothers in America,": National Council on Crime and delinquency San Francisco CA
BMJ, *British Medical Journal* 1996 Personality changes due to "roid rage" published September 21 313-707 http://www.bmj.com/content/313/7059/707.1.extract accessed 2010-12-11
Bosely S. Guardian, Tuesday 29 January (2003) "Prison study could show better diet reduces violence"http://www.guardian.co.uk/society/2008/jan/29/prisonsandprobation.foodanddrink accessed 2010-12-11
Bottoms, A.E. (1999) " Interpersonal Violence and social Order in Prisons;" Crime and Justice; a review of Research, 26,205-283.
Bowlby, J. (1953*) Child Care and the Growth of Love* (based by permission of the World Health Organisation on the Report: Maternal Care and Mental Health), Harmandsworth Penguin.
Bowlby, J. (1973) *Attachment and loss* New York ; Basic Books
Boyd, C. BBC News (2008) Profile: Gary McKinnonhttp://news.bbc.co.uk/1/hi/technology/4715612.stm, accessed 2010-12-11
Bridges G.S (1996) *Criminal Justice, Prison Violence,* California: Pine Forge Press
Browne D.C (2005);http://www.prisonersfamilies.org.uk/uploadedFiles/Information_and_research/Literature%20Review%202005.PDF accessed 2010-12-11
Cabinet Office & Social Exclusion Task Force (2009), Short Study on Women Offenders, London : Cabinet Office
Carlen, P. and Tchaikovsky (1996) "Women's Imprisonment in England and Wales at the End of the Century: Legitimacy, Realities and Utopias." Chapter.10 in Matthews, R. and Francis, P.(eds.) *Prisons*

2000: An International Perspective on the Present state and future of Imprisonment. Basingstoke: Macmillan.
Cavadino, M and Dignan, J. (2006); *Penal Systems A Comparative* Approach, London, Sage.
CCJS (Centre for Criminal Justice Studies) 2007 Report .http://www.publications.parliament.uk/pa/cm200607/cmselect/cmconst/467/467we03.htm accessed 2010-12-11
Change the Record, NACRO http://www.changetherecord.org/about/
Chesney K (1970)*The Victorian Underworld.* St. Giles House London ; Purnell Book Services, Ltd..
Cleckley, H. (1977) The Mask of Sanity, 5th edition, St. Louis : Mosby.
CLINKS Make Every Child Matter - http://www.prisonersfamilies.org.uk/uploadedFiles/Publications_and_resources/ActionNews_Spring%202010_lores.pdf accessed 2010-12-11
Codd, H . 15 June (2007)" Prisoners Families and Resettlement: A Critical Analysis." *The Howard Journal of Criminal Justice*http://onlinelibrary.wiley.com/doi/10.1111/j.1468-2311.2007.00472.x/full accessed 2010-12-11
Cohen, N.The Independent, March 13 (1994).http://www.independent.co.uk/news/courts-jail-845-for-not-paying-tv-licence-fines-1428836.htm accessed 2010-12-11
Condry, R. 2007, *Families Shamed: the Consequences of Crime for Relatives of Serious Offenders.* Cullompton: Willan Publishing.
Corston, Baroness Jean , the Corston Report- *Women in the criminal justice system*, in the Howard Journal of Criminal Justice 13 March 2007
Crime and Disorder Act (1998)http://wapedia.mobi/en/Timeline_of_children%27s_rights_in_the_United_Kingdom. Accessed 2010-12-11
Diamond Project, Wednesday 1 December 2010 Channel 4 News*; Met`s Diamond Project May Cut Reoffending and Save Money.*,channel4.com/news/net/-police-rehabilitation-project-under-threat accessed 2010-12-11
Dickens C. Little Dorrit www.charlesdickenspage.com/dorrit.html 2010-12-11
Dignan, J.(1991)" Repairing the Damage: An Evaluation of an Experimental Adult Reparation Scheme in Kettering Northamptonshire "1987-89, *Sheffield Centre for Criminological and Legal Research, Faculty of Law, University of Sheffield.*
Downing D (1998), *Daylight robbery, the importance of sunlight to health*, Arrow Books.
Engels .F *The Condition of the working Classes in England in* 1844(translated by W. O. Henderson and W. H. Chalenor 1958)
Engels, Frederick (1971) original 1844The *Condition of the working class in England* translated by Henderson and Chalenor, Oxford ; Basil Blackwell.
Every Child Matters.,http://www.google.co.uk/#hl=en&source=hp&biw=826&bih=596&q=every+child+matters+green+paper&aq=9&aqi=g10&aql=&oq=every+child+matters&gs_rfai=&fp=b58b1466451b89c6 accessed 2010-12-11
FFOPS Swansea 101 Mansel St.http://www.ffops.org.uk/index.php?option=com_content&view=category&layout=blog&id=3&Itemid=3 accessed 2010-12-11
Fight Club Thursday - October 7 (2010) http://swns.com/fight-club-prisoners-paid-to-attend-anger-management-classes-071117.html accessed 2010-12-11
Giedd et al (2005) NIMH, "the Adolescent brain, a work in progress." http://www.thenationalcampaign.org/resources/pdf/BRAIN.pdf accessed 2010-12-11
Green Paper "*Tackling Drugs Together*"http://www.drugtext.org/library/articles/four1.html accessed 2010-12-11
Harlow, H.F (1958)".The Nature of Love" *American Psychologist* 13; 673-85 Harlow, H. F. and Zimmerman, R.R. (1959) "Affectional Responses in the Infant Monkey". *Science*130:421-32.
HM Prison Service (2010)http://www.hmprisonservice.gov.uk/resourcecentre/publicationsdocuments/index.asp?cat=85accessed 2010-12-11
Home Office Research and Statistics Directorate- Research findings no, 38http://rds.homeoffice.gov.uk/rds/pdfs/r38.pdfaccessed 2010-12-11
The Howard League for Penal Reform The Howard, Spring (2010).(Offender management caseloads statistics, (2007), 161 Home Office).
Howard, The (Sentencing statistics for England and Wales 2010).
Hoyle, C (ed.) (2009) *Restorative Justice* (critical concepts series), London; Routledge.

INQUEST Statistics, deaths in prisonhttp://inquest.gn.apc.org/data_deaths_in_prison.html
Johnson, A (1995*) Prison culture, violence and sexuality*, Melbourne: Latrobe University press.
Liebling, A (2005) *The Effects of imprisonment.*Cullompton;Willan.
Marx, Karl and Engels, Frederick (1848) *Manifesto of the Communist Party*, in Marx-Engels Selected Works, vol. 1, London; Lawrence and Wishart.
Marx Karl (1904) originally published (1859), *Critique of Political Economy*, New York: International library
McGuire J. (2000*) Cognitive behavioural approaches; an introduction to theory and research*, London, HMIP
McGuire, J. and Priestley, P. (1995) *What Works; Past present and Future*` in McGuire (ed) (1995) *What Works; Reducing Re-offending Guidelines from Research and Practice,* Chichester: John Wiley and Sons.
Murray J. (2007)"The cycle of punishment; social exclusion of prisoners and their children ".*Criminology and Criminal Justice*.7; 55-81.
NACRO" Change the record campaign" 13 September (2010) http://www.nacro.org.uk/news-and-resources/latest-news/campaign-launch,711,NAP.html
PACT, established in 2001 - http://www.prisonadvice.org.uk/?q=pacthistory#housing accessed 2010-12-11
Pantazis,C. & Gordon, D. (1996)."Television licence evasion and the criminalisation of female poverty ", the *Howard Journal*, 36 pp. 170-186.
Prison Timelinehttp://www.institutions.org.uk/prisons/info/prisons_timeline.htmaccessed 2010-12-11
Raynor, P. and Vanstone, M. (1994) Straight Thinking on Probation, Third Interim Evaluation Report: Reconviction within 12 months following STOP Orders, Custodial Sentences and Other Community Sentences, Mid Glamorgan Probation Service.
Reimann, J.(1984) *The rich Get richer and the Poor Get Prison*,4th edition, New York; Macmillan.
Reuters, report by Peter Griffiths July 13 2010
Rutter, M. and Giller, H. (1983), *Juvenile Delinquency trends and perspectives,* Harmandsworth: Penguin.
Shaw, R.(1991) *Prisoners` Children ; What are the issues,*London ; Routledge.
Skinner, B.F.(1972) *Cumulative Record; A selection of Papers*. New York; Appleton-century- Crofts,
Smith, R., Grimshaw, R.,Romeo, R. and Knapp, M. (2007) "Poverty and Disadvantage" .The Joseph Rowntree Foundation.
Sowell et al,(1999)In vivo evidence for post adolescent brain maturation in frontal and striatal regions ; *Nature Neuroscience*,vol. 2 p.859
Swansea Gov Social Inclusion Unit -http://www.swansea.gov.uk/index.cfm?articleid=1449 accessed 2010-12-11
Taser XREPhttp://uk.reuters.com/article/idUKTRE66C3P720100713accessed 2010-12-11
Tosh, J (1982) *The pains of imprisonment*, California; Sage Publications.
Travis, A. Thursday 8 July 2010 Guardian, "Anti-terror stop and search plans to be scrapped"http://www.guardian.co.uk/law/2010/jul/08/anti-terror-stop-and-search-scrapped accessed 2010-12-11
Walker, D. 8 April 2006 BBC News "The Struggle to stay in touch" http://news.bbc.co.uk/1/hi/uk/4735964.stm accessed 2010-12-11
Watson, J.B.(1928) *Psychological care of infant and child*. New York: Norton,
Women against Sharia Law 2010http://womenagainstshariah.blogspot.com/accessed 2010-12-13
Woolf, Lord Justice (1991) Prison Disturbances April 1990: Report of an Enquiry by the Rt. Hon Lord Justice Woolf (parts 1 and 11) and His Honour Judge Stephen Tumin (Part 11), Cm 1456, London HMSO.
Wolpe, J.(1966) *the Practice of Behaviour Therapy*. NewYork Pergamon Press,

Chapter Five

Asch, S. (Asch, S. E. (1951). Effects of group pressure upon the modification and distortion of judgment. In H. Guetzkow (ed.) *Groups, leadership and men*. Pittsburgh, PA: Carnegie Press. (summary here)
Asch, S. E. (1955). Opinions and social pressure *Scientific American, 193*, 31-35.

Asch, S. E. (1956). Studies of independence and conformity: A minority of one against a unanimous majority. *Psychological Monographs, 70* (Whole no. 416).
BBC News (2001) Preaching Caution in Prisons, http://news.bbc.co.uk/1/hi/uk/1730141.stm accessed 2011-02-14
BBC News (July 29 2005) "Do Prisons Radicalise Inmates?"http://news.bbc.co.uk/1/hi/uk/4727723.stm accessed 2011-02-13
Becker, H. S. (1963) *Outsiders: Studies in the Sociology of Deviance,* New York: Free Press

Bond, R., & Smith, P. (1996) Culture and conformity: A meta-analysis of studies using Asch's (1952b, 1956) line judgment task. *Psychological Bulletin*, 119, 111-137.
Bottoms, A .E. (1999) "Interpersonal Violence and Social Order in Prison". *Crime and Justice, 26*: 205-283.
Brisard, J. (2005*) Zarqawi: The New Face of Al-Qaeda,* New York, Other Press.
Clarke, M.(August 2010) "Terrorism in the United Kingdom: Confirming its Modus Operandi", Royal United Services Institute, RUSI.
Cuthbertson, I. (2004) Prisons and the Education of Terrorists*, World Policy Journal,*
Dodd, V. "The Missed danger signals that led to a Brutal Murder" the Guardian, Friday 30 June 2006.
Equality Act 2010 Government Equalities Office, http://www.equalities.gov.uk/equalityact_2010
Forsyth, D. (2006) *Group Dynamics*, 4th edition, Belmont CA: Thomson Wadsworth.

Hamm, M.S.(2009) Prison Islam in the Sacred Age of Terror,*British Journal of Criminology,* vol.49, issue 5 pp. 667-685.
Johnson, A. (1995*) Prison Culture, Violence and Sexuality,*Melbourne: Latrobe University Press
Kohlberg, L. (1981) *Essays on Moral Development,* vol.1: the Philosophy of Moral Development, CA: Harper & Row.
Leppard, D. (2009) "Terrorists Smuggle Fatwas out of Secure Prisons", the Sunday Times, November 15 2009.http://www.timesonline.co.uk/tol/news/uk/article6917296.eceaccessed 2011-02-13
Levi, M. (2007) Organised Crime and Terrorism, in the *Oxford Handbook of Criminology*, 4th ed. , eds. Mike Maguire, Rod Morgan, and Robert Reiner., Oxford: Oxford University Press
Liebling, A.(1992) *Suicides in Prison,* London: Routledge
Liebling, A. (2005) *the Effects of Imprisonment*, Cullompton: Willan.
MacDonald, J.M. (1963) the Threat to Kill, *American Journal of Psychiatry*, 120; 125-130
MacPherson, W. (1999) Stephen Lawrence Inquiry, London: HMSO
Milgram, S. (1963) Behavioural Study of Obedience, *Journal ofAbnormal and Social Psychology*, 67 :371-378.
Milgram, S. (1974) *Obedience to Authority: An Experimental View,* Harper Collins.

Militant Islam Monitor.Org (2005) Paris Metro bomber Algerian Muslim Rachid Ramda to be Extradited from U.K. to France after ten year battlehttp://www.militantislammonitor.org/article/id/1285 accessed 2011-02-14
Moscovici, S., & Zavalloni, M. (1969) "The group as a polarizer of attitudes". *Journal of Personality and Social Psychology*
Neumann, P.R. (2010) "Prisons and Terrorism, Radicalisation and deradicalisation in 15 Countries; A policy report published by the International Centre for the Study of Radicalisation", (ICSR).
Pruitt, D. (1971) Choice shifts in group discussion: An introductory review. *Journal of Personality and Social Psychology, 20*(3), 339-360
Quilliam Report (2009) New Quilliam Report: British Prisons are incubating Islamist Extremismhttp://www.quilliamfoundation.org/index.php/component/content/article/582 accessed 2011-02-13
Rose, D. (2008) "Muslim fanatics to be de-programmed using controversial techniques". http://s10.invisionfree.com/The_Unhived_Mind_II/index.php?showtopic=3218 accessed 2011-02-1
Rothwell, D. J. (1986) Risk-Taking and Polarization in small Group Communication. Communication Education, 35, 172-187.
Seligman, M.E.P. (1975*) Helplessness, on Depression Development and Death,* San Francisco: Freeman.
Seligman, M.E.P. (1977) "Submissive Death; Giving Up on Life",*Psychology Today*, pp. 80-85
Spalek, B. and El-Hassain, S.(2007*)*Prisoner interviews*; Howard Journal of Criminal Justice* 46: 99-114.

Sutherland, E. (1937) *the Professional Thief*, Chicago: University of Chicago Press.
Thomas,J. and Zaitrow, B.H. (2004) "Conning or Conversion; the role of religion in Prison Coping", *The Prison Journal*, 86: 242-59.
Tosh, J. (1982) *the Pains of Imprisonment*, California: Sage Publications.
Warraq, I. (2002) "Virgins: Special Report, Religion in the U.K.", the Guardian, January 12 2002
Wilson, D. and Spalek, B. (2001) Not just visitors to prisons: the experiences of Imams who work inside prisons, *the Howard Journal Of Criminal Justice*, Vol,40, pp. 03-13.
Women against Sharia Law (2010)
Zimbardo, P.G. (1972) "The Stanford Prison Experiment", a slideshow presented by Philip G. Zimbardo, Inc., P.O.Box 4395, Stanford, California 94305 (b).

Chapter Six: Too Mad for Prison?

Babiak, P. and Hare R.D.(2006), *Snakes in Suits: When Psychopaths Go To Work*, New York: Harper Collins.
Barton,A. (2003) *Illicit Drugs*, London: Routledge.
Bean, P. (2008) *Drugs and Crime*, Cullompton: Willan.
BMJ, *British Medical Journal* 1996 Personality changes due to "roid rage" published September 21 313-707 http://www.bmj.com/content/313/7059/707.1.extract accesed 2011-02-26
Buss, D. M. (2005) *The Murderer Next Door: Why the Mind is Designed to Kill*. New York: Penguin Press
Cleckley, H. (1977) *The Mask of Sanity* 5th edition, St. Louis: Mosby
Conway, R. (1994) "Abuse and Intellectual disability: a Potential Link or an Inescapable Reality?" *Australian and New Zealand Journal of Developmental Disabilities*. Vol 19:3, pp. 165-171.
Corston, Baroness, the Corston Report- 13 March 2007- Women in the Criminal Justice System. *The Howard Journal of Criminal Justice* .
Darwin, C. (1872 a) *The Origin of Species*, New York: Macmillan, 6th edition, 1962
Dawkins, R. (1989) *the Selfish Gene*, Oxford, OUP.
DePauw, K. W. and Szulecka, T. K. (1988) "Dangerous Delusions, Violence and the Misidentification Syndromes",*British Journal of Psychiatry*, Vol. 152, pp. 91 -96.
Dobash, R.E., and Dobash, R. D (1979) *Violence against Wives*, New York; Free Press.
Dobash, R.E. and Dobash, R.D. (1992) *Women, Violence and social change*, London; Routledge
The Equality Act (1 October 2010) Government Equalities Office, http://www.equalities.gov.uk/equality_act_2010.aspx accessed 2011-02-26
Eronen, M. Tilhonen, J. and Hakola, P. (1996) "Schizophrenia and Homicidal Behaviour", *Schizophrenia Bulletin*, Vol. 22, pp. 83-89.
Freud, S. (1933) *New introductory lectures on Psychoanalysis*, translated by Strachey, J. New York: Norton 1965.
Freud, S. (1940) *An outline of psychoanalysis*, translated by Srachey, J.

New York: Norton 1970

Giedd et al (2005) NIMH, "the adolescent brain, a work in progress."

http://www.thenationalcampaign.org/resources/pdf/BRAIN.pdf

Hare, R. D. (1993) *Without Conscience: the Disturbing World of Psychopaths Among Us*, New York: Pocket Books.
Hare, R. D. (2003) *Manual for the Revised Psychopathy Checklist* (2nd edition) Toronto, Canada Multi Health Systems.
Laing, R.D. (1960) *the Divided Self: An Existential Study in Sanity and*

Madness. Harmondsworth: Penguin.

Laing, R.D. (1961) *the Self and Others.* London: Tavistock Publications.

Laing, R.D. and Esterson, A. (1964) *Sanity, Madness and the Family.*

London: Penguin Books.

MacDonald, J.M. (1963) the Threat to Kill, *American Journal of Psychiatry*, 120; 125-130
Messerschmidt, J. W. (1993*), Masculinities and Crime.*Lanham, MD; Rowman and Littlefield..
Messerschmidt, J.W (2000) Becoming real men; adolescent masculinity challenges and sexual violence, *Men & Masculinities*, 2 (3), pp.266-307.

Monahan, J., Steadman, H., Silver, E., Appelbaum, P., Robbins, P., Mulvey, E., Roth, L., Grisso, T., & Banks, S. (2001) *Rethinking Risk Assessment: The MacArthur Study of Mental Disorder and Violence.* New York: Oxford University Press.
Nadien, M. B. (1995) Elder Violence (Maltreatment) in Domestic Settings: Some Theory and Research" in Adler and Denmark (eds) Violence and the Prevention of Violence, Westport USA: Greenwood Publishing Group.
Rosenhan, D.L (January 1973) "On being Sane in Insane Places"

Science (New York, N.Y.) **179** (70): 250–8.
Sacks, O. W. (1985) *The Man who mistook his Wife for a Hatt*
Touchstone Books

Seligman, M.E.P. (1975*) Helplessness, On Depression Development and Death.* San Francisco; Freeman.
Seligman, M. E. P (1977) Submissive Death; Giving up on Life. *Psychology Today* pp. 80-85.
Sowell et al, (1999)"In vivo evidence for post adolescent brain maturation in frontal and striatal regions" ; *Nature Neuroscience* ,vol. 2 p.859
Steadman, H.J. and Keveles, G. (1972) "The Community Adjustment and criminal activity of the Baxstrom Patients" : 1966-1970, *American Journal of Psychiatry* 129:304-310, September 1972

Szasz, T.S. (1960) the Myth of Mental Illness, *AmericanPsychologist,*15,

pp. 113-118.

Szasz, T. S. (1963) *Law, liberty and Psychiatry*, New York: Macmillan.

Taylor, P.J. and Gunn, J. (1999) "Homicides by People with Mental Illness" *British Journal of Psychiatry*, Vol. 174, pp. 9-14.

Wolf, R.S. (1998) "Domestic Elder Abuse and Neglect" in Nordus and

VandenBos (eds) *Clinical Geropsychology, American Psychological*

Society. Washington DC USA

Printed in Poland
by Amazon Fulfillment
Poland Sp. z o.o., Wrocław